Fantastic Filled
CUPCAKES

Fantastic Filled CUPCAKES

Kick Your Baking Up a Notch with Incredible Flavor Combinations

Camila Hurst

Creator of Pies and Tacos

PAGE STREET
PUBLISHING CO.

PAGE STREET
PUBLISHING CO.

First published in 2020 by

Page Street Publishing Co.

27 Congress Street, Suite 1511

Salem, MA 01970

www.pagestreetpublishing.com

Distributed by Macmillan, sales in Canada by The Canadian Manda Group.

25 24 23 22   4 5 6 7

ISBN-13: 978-1-64567-166-4

ISBN-10: 1-64567-166-6

Library of Congress Control Number: 2019957320

Cover and book design by Ashley Tenn for Page Street Publishing Co.

Photography by Camila Hurst

Printed and bound in the United States

Page Street Publishing protects our planet by donating to nonprofits like The Trustees, which focuses on local land conservation.

This book is dedicated to
MY SON, LUKE, WHO IS THE SWEETEST BOY IN THE WHOLE WORLD.

Table of Contents

INTRODUCTION

Welcome to *Fantastic Filled Cupcakes*, the place where all of your sweet cupcake dreams come true! There is absolutely nothing modest about the cupcakes you will find in this book. Even the easiest ones to make are eye-catching, unquestionably enticing and tasty, beginning with the fact that they are all filled! Fifty-four cupcake recipes with delicious fillings, including custard, fudge, caramel, jams, curds and more, are waiting for you in the pages of this book! Just the beautiful presentation of the cupcakes alone will be enough to grab your attention, and after the first bite, you will be convinced that every cupcake you have from now on should be filled with something fantastic too!

I got acquainted with baking at a very early age, as I grew up in my grandma's bakery, right down the street from my house in Brazil. She built and ran the bakery for fifty years and woke up before the sun every day to bake fresh bread that was enjoyed by everyone in our neighborhood. One of my best memories is watching my grandma make tart shells; she was always so meticulous and gentle with the pastries, really taking her time with each one. I learned a lot from her dedication and commitment to her craft.

I've tried to emulate that attention to detail and her desire to captivate and please her customers in my own baking. I am a firm believer that we eat with our eyes first, so when making any dessert, my approach is always to try to make them striking and appealing. And I trust that you will find that to be true as you create the recipes in this book. I always strive to make sweets that belong in a beautiful bakery case, just like my grandma's.

As I was learning how to bake by myself, and getting creative in the kitchen, I found out how cupcakes can be a great canvas for creating beautiful treats, because they are versatile, often easier to make and decorate than cakes and, let's face it, more fun to enjoy as well. I also found that making filled cupcakes provides the baker with a great opportunity for adding more layers of texture, flavor and enjoyment to this popular dessert. The fillings make the cupcakes more complex, inviting and impressive. I love to create over-the-top cupcakes that are dressed up from top to bottom and include a delicious surprise inside and a special treat adorning the top, adding to their dazzling and whimsical look.

That's my definition of going the extra mile, which is not only an attitude I carry about baking cupcakes but also about every aspect of my life. Naturally, that approach shows through in every detail of this special book. Each recipe here was cheerfully imagined and carefully tested, and I have thoroughly enjoyed every step of this process, from baking the cupcakes to photographing and then devouring them!

My intention with this book is that you also get to experience what it means to go above and beyond and bake something truly unique and awe-inspiring. I hope you'll see how rewarding it is to spread cheer and joy to the world through sharing these delightful creations with family, friends and neighbors to sweeten up their lives. I hope this book will open up a new realm of cupcake delight for you.

Camila Hurst

Chocolate Lovers

Calling all chocolate lovers! The recipes in this chapter were specially written for you, by a chocolate lover herself! From traditional combinations, such as coconut and chocolate in the Chocolate Coconut Macaroon Cupcakes (page 33), to newer trends like the Caramelized White Chocolate Almond Cupcakes (page 37), you will find that the following filled cupcakes satisfy all of your deepest chocolate cravings.

Chocolate is one of my favorite ingredients to bake with, and you will find more chocolate recipes in other chapters as well. So don't think that it stops here! There are plenty more rich chocolate recipes to indulge in and enjoy throughout the book.

If you are just starting your filled-cupcake adventure and are wondering where to begin, any recipe from this chapter would probably be a good place to start because chocolate is always a no-brainer!

CHOCOLATE ORANGE MACADAMIA CUPCAKES

I am still trying to find a combination that works better together than chocolate and orange. Add macadamias to the mix and you've got yourself a fierce trio. Rich and fluffy Chocolate Cupcakes are filled with a citrusy Orange Marmalade, topped with creamy Macadamia Buttercream and garnished with Orange-Glazed Macadamia Nuts to take this magnificent recipe over the top.

Makes 14 cupcakes

CHOCOLATE CUPCAKES

1½ cups (190 g) all-purpose flour

¼ cup (31 g) unsweetened cocoa powder

1 tsp espresso powder (optional)

1 tsp baking soda

¾ tsp baking powder

½ tsp fine sea salt

½ cup (120 ml) canola oil

1 cup (200 g) granulated sugar

1 cup (240 ml) brewed coffee or hot water

1 tbsp (15 ml) white vinegar

2 tsp (10 ml) vanilla extract

ORANGE MARMALADE

2 cups (280 g) peeled and chopped oranges

¼ cup (60 ml) water

½ cup (100 g) granulated sugar

2 tbsp (10 g) orange zest

To make the Chocolate Cupcakes, preheat the oven to 350°F (177°C) and line 14 cupcake tins with cupcake liners. Line a baking sheet with a silicone mat or parchment paper.

In a large bowl, sift together the flour, cocoa powder, espresso powder (if using), baking soda, baking powder and salt; set aside.

In another bowl, mix the oil, granulated sugar, coffee, vinegar and vanilla. Pour the dry mixture over the wet ingredients and whisk briefly, until incorporated. Be careful not to overmix. As soon as you see no more streaks of dry mixture, stop whisking.

Divide the batter evenly among the cupcake liners, filling them about two-thirds of the way. Bake the cupcakes for about 18 minutes. Start checking the cupcakes at the 15-minute mark, and keep baking and checking as necessary. To see if the cupcakes are ready, gently press with your finger on top of the cupcakes, and if they spring right back, that means they are done baking. Let the cupcakes cool completely before filling and frosting.

To make the Orange Marmalade, place the chopped oranges, water, granulated sugar and orange zest in a small saucepan over medium heat. Bring the mixture to a boil, then lower the heat to medium-low. Stir the oranges regularly as you let them cook for about 40 minutes. If the marmalade begins to get dry, lower the heat and add 1 teaspoon of water or a splash of citrus juice (lemon or orange) and continue to cook until the mixture looks thick and glossy. Remove the marmalade from the heat and let it cool. You may enjoy it as-is or process it in the blender to make it smoother.

(continued)

MACADAMIA BUTTERCREAM

1 cup (120 g) macadamia nuts

¾ cup (170 g) unsalted butter, at room temperature

2½ to 3½ cups (312 to 437 g) powdered sugar, sifted

1 tbsp (15 ml) milk, if needed

ORANGE-GLAZED MACADAMIA NUTS

1 cup (120 g) macadamia nuts

½ cup (100 g) granulated sugar

3 tbsp (45 ml) orange juice

2 tbsp (10 g) orange zest

To make the Macadamia Buttercream, place the macadamia nuts in a small blender or food processor and process until they are finely ground. You may have to do this in batches. Process for a bit, and then remove the macadamias that are already ground from the blender, leaving the large pieces in. Then process the larger pieces until they are also ground. You don't want huge pieces of macadamias in the buttercream, because that might make it hard to frost the cupcakes later.

Next, place the butter in a large bowl and cream with an electric mixer on medium-high speed for 4 minutes. Turn the mixer off, add the sifted powdered sugar and mix on low speed until combined, then increase the speed to medium-high and beat for another minute, until creamy. Add the milk only if the buttercream is too stiff. If the buttercream has a runny consistency, add more powdered sugar.

To make the Orange-Glazed Macadamia Nuts, place the macadamia nuts, granulated sugar, orange juice and zest in a small saucepan over medium heat. Bring the mixture to a boil while stirring frequently. Reduce the heat and let the nuts and syrup simmer gently. Slowly the syrup will become thick like caramel. The total cooking time will be around 5 minutes. The syrup should look glossy and coat the macadamias with a thick layer. Spread the nuts on the prepared baking sheet. Let the nuts dry for a few hours. Break them apart as desired. Store any leftover nuts in an airtight container for up to 5 days.

To assemble the cupcakes, use a spoon to remove the center of each cupcake. Spoon some of the Orange Marmalade into the middle of the cupcakes. Place the Macadamia Buttercream in a piping bag fitted with the piping tip of choice. Pipe the frosting over the cupcakes. Top each cupcake with some Orange-Glazed Macadamia Nuts.

The cupcakes can be stored in the refrigerator, covered, for up to 4 days.

CHOCOLATE HAZELNUT PRALINE CUPCAKES

These Chocolate Hazelnut Praline Cupcakes are for chocolate lovers as well as caramel lovers and hazelnut lovers. I am all three of those things, so needless to say I love every bite of them! From the fluffy Chocolate Cupcakes, which are filled with a silky Hazelnut Caramel Sauce, to the super-rich Chocolate Frosting, these cupcakes are perfectly sweet and indulgent. And the best part is they come with a treat: Hazelnut Praline Candy on top, which is so easy to make! Deliciousness from the bottom to the top!

Makes 14 cupcakes

CHOCOLATE CUPCAKES

1½ cups (190 g) all-purpose flour

¼ cup (31 g) unsweetened cocoa powder

1 tsp espresso powder (optional)

1 tsp baking soda

¾ tsp baking powder

½ tsp fine sea salt

½ cup (120 ml) canola oil

1 cup (200 g) granulated sugar

1 cup (240 ml) brewed coffee or hot water

1 tbsp (15 ml) white vinegar

2 tsp (10 ml) vanilla extract

HAZELNUT CARAMEL SAUCE

¼ cup (32 g) whole roasted hazelnuts

⅓ cup (66 g) granulated sugar

1½ tbsp (21 g) unsalted butter

2½ tbsp (37 ml) heavy cream

¼ tsp salt (optional for salted caramel)

To make the Chocolate Cupcakes, preheat the oven to 350°F (177°C) and line 14 cupcake tins with cupcake liners. Line a baking sheet with parchment paper.

In a large bowl, sift together the flour, cocoa powder, espresso powder (if using), baking soda, baking powder and salt; set aside. In another bowl, mix together the oil, granulated sugar, coffee, vinegar and vanilla. Pour the dry mixture over the wet ingredients and whisk briefly until incorporated. Be careful not to overmix. As soon as you see no more streaks of dry mixture, stop whisking.

Divide the batter evenly among the cupcake liners, filling the cups about two-thirds of the way. Bake the cupcakes for about 18 minutes. Start checking the cupcakes at the 15-minute mark, and keep baking and checking as necessary. To see if the cupcakes are ready, gently press with your finger on top of the cupcakes, and if they spring right back, that means they are done baking. Let the cupcakes cool completely before filling and frosting.

To make the Hazelnut Caramel Sauce, grind the hazelnuts to very tiny bits in a food processor. You may also chop them with a knife if you want to, but be sure to chop them very small. Set the nuts aside.

Melt the granulated sugar in a small saucepan over medium heat, stirring frequently so the sugar melts evenly. Once all the sugar has melted, and you see no more bits of sugar granules in the pan, it should have a light brown color. Remove the pan from the heat and add the butter and heavy cream. Be very careful when doing this because the mixture will bubble up and splatter. Immediately start to stir the caramel vigorously; place it over low heat for 1 to 2 minutes, still stirring, to re-melt the sugar that crystallized when you added the cream and butter.

(continued)

CHOCOLATE FROSTING

1 cup (170 g) chopped chocolate or chocolate chips

1½ cups (187 g) powdered sugar

¼ cup (31 g) cocoa powder

1 cup (226 g) unsalted butter, at room temperature

1 tsp vanilla extract

HAZELNUT PRALINE CANDY

¾ cup (150 g) granulated sugar

¾ cup (150 g) packed brown sugar

½ cup (120 ml) evaporated milk

2 tbsp (28 g) unsalted butter

1 cup (128 g) whole roasted hazelnuts

Once the caramel is smooth, remove it from the heat, add the ground hazelnuts and stir to combine. Stir in the salt, if using. Pour the caramel into a bowl and let it come to room temperature before using it to fill the cupcakes. Don't place it in the fridge or the caramel might become too hard to scoop to fill the cupcakes.

To make the Chocolate Frosting, place the chocolate in a microwave-safe bowl and melt it in the microwave at 15-second intervals, stirring in between, until completely melted and smooth. Let it cool to room temperature.

In a large bowl, sift together the powdered sugar and cocoa powder. In another bowl, beat the butter with an electric mixer on medium-high speed for 4 minutes, until fluffy and whitened in color. Turn the mixer off and add the sifted mixture. Mix on low speed to combine. Increase the speed to medium and beat for 1 more minute. Add the melted and cooled chocolate to the bowl. Mix until incorporated, scraping the sides of the bowl if necessary. Add the vanilla and mix to combine.

If the frosting seems runny, add more sifted powdered sugar until you achieve the desired consistency. If the frosting seems stiff, add 1 teaspoon of milk at a time, stirring in between, until you achieve the perfect consistency. Keep the frosting covered until you are ready to frost the cupcakes.

To make the Hazelnut Praline Candy, add the granulated sugar, brown sugar and evaporated milk to a small saucepan. Bring to a boil over medium heat, stirring frequently, until the mixture achieves the thread stage, or a candy thermometer registers 225°F (107°C). Remove the pan from the heat, add the butter and hazelnuts, return the pan to the heat and keep cooking while stirring until the mixture achieves the soft ball stage, or a candy thermometer registers 235°F (112°C).

Immediately remove the pan from the heat and use a spatula to stir the mixture vigorously until it begins to thicken as it cools ever so slightly, about 1 minute. Quickly drop mounds of 1 tablespoon (15 g) of hazelnuts onto the prepared baking sheet. The hazelnuts should have a heavy coating of the thick sauce around them. Be sure to work fast, because the mixture will start to set very quickly. Let it dry completely for a couple of hours.

To assemble the cupcakes, make a hole in the center of each cupcake using a spoon. Spoon some of the Hazelnut Caramel Sauce into the middle of the cupcakes. Place the Chocolate Frosting in a piping bag fitted with the tip of choice and pipe the frosting on top of the cupcakes. Top each cupcake with a Hazelnut Praline Candy.

The cupcakes can be stored in the refrigerator, covered, for up to 4 days. Be sure to let them come to room temperature slightly before serving, so the caramel filling has a chance to soften up a bit.

DARK CHOCOLATE CHERRY CUPCAKES

The combination of dark chocolate and cherries is so inviting and romantic. This is a very rich and scrumptious combo that will delight and captivate your taste buds. The tart Cherry Jam filling, the bold Chocolate Cupcakes and the sweet and creamy Cherry Buttercream are topped off with Chocolate-Dipped Cherries, which are literally the cherry on top of this delicious creation.

Makes 14 cupcakes

CHOCOLATE CUPCAKES

1½ cups (190 g) all-purpose flour

¼ cup (31 g) unsweetened cocoa powder

1 tsp espresso powder (optional)

1 tsp baking soda

¾ tsp baking powder

½ tsp fine sea salt

½ cup (120 ml) canola oil

1 cup (200 g) granulated sugar

1 cup (240 ml) brewed coffee or hot water

1 tbsp (15 ml) white vinegar

2 tsp (10 ml) vanilla extract

CHERRY JAM

2 cups (300 g) cherries, pitted

2 tbsp (25 g) granulated sugar

2 tbsp (30 ml) lemon juice

1 tsp cornstarch

2 tsp (10 ml) water

To make the Chocolate Cupcakes, preheat the oven to 350°F (177°C) and line 14 cupcake tins with cupcake liners. Line a baking sheet with a silicone mat or parchment paper.

In a large bowl, sift together the flour, cocoa powder, espresso powder (if using), baking soda, baking powder and salt; set aside.

In another bowl, mix together the oil, granulated sugar, coffee, vinegar and vanilla. Pour the dry mixture over the wet ingredients and whisk briefly until incorporated. Be careful not to overmix. As soon as you see no more streaks of dry mixture, stop whisking.

Divide the batter evenly among the cupcake liners, filling them about two-thirds of the way. Bake the cupcakes for about 18 minutes. Start checking the cupcakes at the 15-minute mark, and keep baking and checking as necessary. To see if the cupcakes are ready, gently press with your finger on top of the cupcakes, and if they spring right back, that means they are done baking. Let the cupcakes cool completely before filling and frosting.

To make the Cherry Jam, place the cherries, granulated sugar and lemon juice in a small saucepan over medium heat and cook for about 15 minutes, until the cherries have softened. Be sure to stir the mixture every so often, and if it's getting too dry as it cooks, add 1 teaspoon of water and lower the heat. In a small bowl, mix the cornstarch with the water until dissolved, then add it to the pan with the softened cherries. Keep stirring and cooking until the jam thickens, about 2 minutes. Let the jam cool slightly, for about 5 minutes, and then place it in a small food processor or blender and blend until smooth. Transfer the jam to a bowl, cover it and refrigerate until thoroughly chilled.

(continued)

CHERRY BUTTERCREAM

¾ cup (170 g) unsalted butter,
at room temperature

2¾ cups (340 g) powdered sugar,
sifted

2 tbsp (30 ml) Cherry Jam

CHOCOLATE-DIPPED CHERRIES

14 pitted cherries

⅓ cup (56 g) chopped dark chocolate
or chocolate chips

To make the Cherry Buttercream, in a bowl, beat the butter with an electric mixer on medium-high speed for 4 minutes. Turn the mixer off, add the sifted powdered sugar and mix on low speed to combine. Increase the speed to medium and beat for 1 minute. Add the Cherry Jam to the bowl and cream again, scraping the bowl if necessary. If the buttercream is runny, add a bit more sifted powdered sugar. If the buttercream seems too stiff, add 1 teaspoon of water or milk at a time to adjust the consistency.

To make the Chocolate-Dipped Cherries, rinse the cherries, then dry them well and set aside. Place the chocolate in a small microwave-safe bowl. Microwave the chocolate in 20-second intervals, stirring in between, until completely melted and smooth. Dip each cherry into the melted chocolate, and then place them on the prepared baking sheet. Let the chocolate dry completely. You can place the cherries in the fridge to speed up this process.

To assemble the cupcakes, remove the center of each cupcake with a spoon. Spoon some Cherry Jam into the center of each cupcake. Place the Cherry Buttercream in a piping bag fitted with the tip of choice and pipe over each cupcake. Top with a Chocolate-Dipped Cherry.

The cupcakes can be stored in the refrigerator, covered, for up to 4 days. Let them come to room temperature slightly before serving.

MIXED BERRY CHOCOLATE CUPCAKES

When you try one of these Mixed Berry Chocolate Cupcakes, you get the richness of the Chocolate Cupcakes, the tartness of the Mixed Berries Jam and the light, sweet taste of the Vanilla Bean Mascarpone Frosting. It's a heavenly combination of flavors and textures that complement and energize each other, and you will experience the harmony of these elements in each bite.

Makes 14 cupcakes

CHOCOLATE CUPCAKES

1½ cups (190 g) all-purpose flour

¼ cup (31 g) unsweetened cocoa powder

1 tsp espresso powder (optional)

1 tsp baking soda

¾ tsp baking powder

½ tsp fine sea salt

½ cup (120 ml) canola oil

1 cup (200 g) granulated sugar

1 cup (240 ml) brewed coffee or hot water

1 tbsp (15 ml) white vinegar

2 tsp (10 ml) vanilla extract

MIXED BERRIES JAM

2 cups (240 g) mixed berries, plus more for decorating (optional)

2 tbsp (25 g) granulated sugar

2 tbsp (30 ml) lemon juice

1 tsp cornstarch

2 tsp (10 ml) water

To make the Chocolate Cupcakes, preheat the oven to 350°F (177°C) and line 14 cupcake tins with cupcake liners.

In a large bowl, sift together the flour, cocoa powder, espresso powder (if using), baking soda, baking powder and salt; set aside.

In another bowl, mix together the oil, granulated sugar, coffee, vinegar and vanilla. Pour the dry mixture over the wet ingredients and whisk briefly until incorporated. Be careful not to overmix. As soon as you see no more streaks of dry mixture, stop whisking.

Divide the batter evenly among the cupcake liners, filling them about two-thirds of the way. Bake the cupcakes for about 18 minutes. Start checking the cupcakes at the 15-minute mark, and keep baking and checking as necessary. To see if the cupcakes are ready, gently press with your finger on top of the cupcakes, and if they spring right back, that means they are done baking. Let the cupcakes cool completely before filling and frosting.

To make the Mixed Berries Jam, you can use a combination of your favorite berries such as raspberries, blueberries and strawberries. If using large berries such as strawberries, chop them into quarters first. Place the berries, granulated sugar and lemon juice in a small saucepan over medium heat and cook for about 15 minutes, until the berries have softened. Be sure to stir the mixture every so often, and if it's getting too dry as it cooks, add 1 teaspoon of water and lower the heat.

In a small bowl, mix the cornstarch with the water until dissolved, then add it to the pan. Keep stirring and cooking the jam until it thickens, about 2 minutes. Transfer the jam to a bowl, cover and refrigerate until thoroughly chilled.

(continued)

VANILLA BEAN MASCARPONE FROSTING

1 cup (240 ml) heavy cream, cold

1 vanilla bean (see Note)

¾ cup (93 g) powdered sugar, sifted

1 cup (226 g) mascarpone cheese, cold

To make the Vanilla Bean Mascarpone Frosting, whip the heavy cream in a large bowl with an electric mixer on medium-high speed for 1 to 2 minutes, until soft peaks form. Slice the vanilla bean in half and use the back of a paring knife to scrape the seeds into the bowl with the heavy cream.

Add the sifted powdered sugar to the bowl and mix briefly until combined. Add the mascarpone cheese to the bowl and whip on medium-high speed for 2 minutes, or until you obtain stiff peaks. The frosting is best if piped immediately after it is made, but it will hold its shape pretty well once piped for a few days.

To assemble the cupcakes, use a spoon to remove the center of each cupcake. Spoon some of the Mixed Berries Jam into the middle of each cupcake. Place the Vanilla Bean Mascarpone Frosting in a piping bag fitted with the tip of choice. Pipe the frosting on top of the cupcakes. You can decorate each cupcake with fresh berries, if desired.

The cupcakes can be stored in the refrigerator, covered, for up to 4 days.

Note: If you don't want to use vanilla bean, substitute for 1 teaspoon of vanilla extract and add it to the frosting once you've creamed the mascarpone cheese in. Mix briefly to combine.

FLOURLESS CHOCOLATE BLACKBERRY CUPCAKES

What I love the most about these Flourless Chocolate Blackberry Cupcakes is the incredible richness and texture of the Flourless Chocolate Cupcakes. They pair so well with the tangy Blackberry Jam filling, which is also used to color the Blackberry Buttercream to top the cupcakes. This recipe is so easy to make and sure to be a crowd-pleaser!

Makes 10 cupcakes

FLOURLESS CHOCOLATE CUPCAKES

½ cup (87 g) semisweet chocolate chips or chopped chocolate

½ cup (113 g) unsalted butter

⅔ cup (132 g) packed brown sugar

½ tsp fine sea salt

3 large eggs, at room temperature

⅔ cup (85 g) unsweetened cocoa powder

¼ tsp espresso powder (optional)

BLACKBERRY JAM

1½ cups (216 g) blackberries, plus extra for decorating (optional)

3 tbsp (37 g) granulated sugar

2 tbsp (30 ml) lemon juice (about 1 lemon)

1 tsp cornstarch

2 tsp (10 ml) water

To make the Flourless Chocolate Cupcakes, preheat the oven to 375°F (190°C). Line 10 cupcake tins with paper liners and set aside.

Place the chocolate and butter in a microwave-safe bowl. Microwave for 15-second intervals, stirring in between, until the chocolate and butter are melted. Transfer to a large bowl. Add the brown sugar and salt and whisk until smooth.

Add the eggs, one at a time, whisking each egg until completely incorporated before adding the next one. Sift the cocoa powder and espresso powder (if using) on top, and whisk until incorporated.

Divide the batter among the cupcake liners, filling them about three-fourths of the way. Bake for 12 to 15 minutes, until you can touch the top of the cupcakes and they spring back instead of sinking in. Let them cool completely before filling and frosting.

To make the Blackberry Jam, place the blackberries, granulated sugar and lemon juice in a small saucepan over medium-low heat and cook for 10 to 15 minutes, until the blackberries have fallen apart. Strain 2 tablespoons (30 ml) of jam to be used in the buttercream later. You can also strain all of the jam if you don't want any seeds in the jam filling.

In a small bowl, mix the cornstarch and water, and then add it to the pan with the blackberries. Cook for a couple of minutes, stirring, until thick.

(continued)

BLACKBERRY BUTTERCREAM

¾ cup (170 g) unsalted butter, at room temperature

2¾ cups (340 g) powdered sugar, sifted

2 tbsp (30 ml) Blackberry Jam

To make the Blackberry Buttercream, in a bowl, beat the butter with an electric mixer on medium-high speed for 4 minutes. Turn the mixer off and add the sifted powdered sugar, then mix on low speed to combine. Increase the speed to medium and beat for 1 minute. Add the Blackberry Jam and cream again, scraping the bowl if necessary, until well combined. If the buttercream is runny, add a bit more sifted powdered sugar in. If the buttercream seems too stiff, add 1 teaspoon of water or milk at a time to adjust the consistency.

To assemble the cupcakes, remove the center of each cupcake with a spoon. Spoon some jam into the center of each cupcake. Place the Blackberry Buttercream in a piping bag fitted with the tip of choice and pipe on top of the cupcakes. To decorate, top with a blackberry, if desired.

The cupcakes can be stored in the refrigerator, covered, for up to 4 days. Let them come to room temperature slightly before serving.

Note: You can also use store-bought jam for this recipe. You will need about ⅔ cup (160 g) of jam to fill the cupcakes and about 2 tablespoons (30 g) of jam for the buttercream.

CHOCOLATE COCONUT MACAROON CUPCAKES

These Chocolate Coconut Macaroon Cupcakes are perfect for chocolate lovers as well as coconut lovers. They are filled and topped with a silky Chocolate Coconut Pastry Cream, which is smooth and not overly sweet, offering the perfect balance to the richness of the chocolate cupcake. Add the chewy, toothsome Chocolate Coconut Macaroon on top and you have a showstopper. If you love the combo of chocolate and coconut, these cupcakes are for you!

Makes 14 cupcakes

CHOCOLATE CUPCAKES

1½ cups (190 g) all-purpose flour

¼ cup (31 g) unsweetened cocoa powder

1 tsp espresso powder (optional)

1 tsp baking soda

¾ tsp baking powder

½ tsp fine sea salt

½ cup (120 ml) canola oil

1 cup (200 g) granulated sugar

1 cup (240 ml) brewed coffee or hot water

1 tbsp (15 ml) white vinegar

2 tsp (10 ml) vanilla extract

To make the Chocolate Cupcakes, preheat the oven to 350°F (177°C). In a large bowl, sift together the flour, cocoa powder, espresso powder (if using), baking soda, baking powder and salt; set aside.

In another bowl, mix together the oil, granulated sugar, coffee, vinegar and vanilla. Pour the dry mixture over the wet ingredients and whisk briefly until incorporated. Be careful not to overmix. As soon as you see no more streaks of dry mixture, stop whisking.

Divide the batter evenly among the cupcake liners, filling them about two-thirds of the way. Bake the cupcakes for about 18 minutes. Start checking the cupcakes at the 15-minute mark, and keep baking and checking as necessary. To see if the cupcakes are ready, gently press with your finger on top of the cupcakes, and if they spring right back, that means they are done baking. Let the cupcakes cool completely before filling and frosting.

(continued)

CHOCOLATE COCONUT PASTRY CREAM

1½ cups (360 ml) coconut milk or whole milk

3 large egg yolks

⅔ cup (160 ml) condensed milk or sub for ½ cup (100 g) granulated sugar

1 tbsp (7 g) cocoa powder

2 tbsp (16 g) cornstarch

¼ tsp fine sea salt

⅔ cup (113 g) chopped dark chocolate

1 tsp vanilla extract

1 tbsp (14 g) unsalted butter

½ cup (56 g) shredded coconut

To make the Chocolate Coconut Pastry Cream, place the coconut milk in a small saucepan over medium heat and bring it to almost a boil. Once you see the first bubbles forming, turn off the heat.

Meanwhile, in a bowl, whisk the egg yolks and condensed milk (or sugar) until light in color and very well combined. Add the cocoa powder, cornstarch and salt and whisk until incorporated.

Now it's time to temper the eggs. Slowly pour about ½ cup (120 ml) of the hot milk over the egg mixture while whisking nonstop. Then, slowly add the remaining hot milk to the mixture. Do this slowly, while whisking, so the egg yolks don't get cooked.

Pour this custard back into the saucepan where you heated the milk. You can pour it through a sieve, so you can catch any little bits of egg that may have cooked during the tempering process. Over medium heat, mix the custard with a spatula, nonstop. The custard will slowly start to thicken. At first it will get very lumpy; just trust the process and keep stirring quickly while it cooks and watch it become smooth and creamy. Once the custard is thick and creamy, add the chopped dark chocolate and stir until the chocolate melts. Remove from the heat and stir in the vanilla and butter.

Remove ⅓ cup (80 ml) of the pastry cream to a small bowl, and mix with the shredded coconut. Place a piece of plastic wrap directly on the surface of the custard and place it in the fridge. Pour the remaining chocolate pastry cream without the coconut into another bowl; this will be used to frost the cupcakes later. Cover its surface directly with plastic wrap also, and place it in the fridge.

(continued)

CHOCOLATE COCONUT MACAROONS

⅓ cup plus 1 tbsp (70 g) chopped dark chocolate

⅔ cup (160 ml) condensed milk

1 cup (113 g) shredded coconut (I used unsweetened)

½ tsp vanilla extract

1 large egg white

½ cup (85 g) chopped dark chocolate (for dipping the bottom of the macaroons)

To make the Chocolate Coconut Macaroons, preheat the oven to 325°F (162°C). In a microwave-safe bowl, melt the dark chocolate in the microwave in 15-second intervals, stirring in between until completely melted. Add the condensed milk, stirring until incorporated. Add the shredded coconut and vanilla and stir.

In a separate bowl, whip the egg white with an electric mixer until stiff peaks form. Add the whipped egg white to the condensed milk mixture, and fold with a rubber spatula until it is incorporated.

Use a cookie scoop to form balls and place them on the prepared baking sheet. This recipe makes 20 to 30 macaroons depending on how big you make them. The perfect size to top the cupcakes is about 1½ teaspoons (7 g) of dough, and they will rise slightly when they bake.

Bake for 10 to 15 minutes. They should still be soft, but set, when you remove them from the oven. Don't overbake the macaroons or they will become dry and tough. Let them cool completely.

Once the macaroons are cool, melt the chocolate in a microwave-safe bowl and dip each macaroon bottom into the melted chocolate. Place them on a piece of parchment paper to set. You can also put some of the chocolate in a piping bag or use a spoon to drizzle some chocolate on top of the cookies. Leftover macaroons will keep in an airtight container for up to 1 week at room temperature.

To assemble the cupcakes, use a spoon to remove the center of each cooled cupcake. Spoon some of the Chocolate Coconut Pastry Cream into the middle of each cupcake. Place the plain Chocolate Pastry Cream in a piping bag fitted with the tip of choice, and pipe it over the cupcakes. To decorate, place a Chocolate Coconut Macaroon on top.

The cupcakes can be stored in the refrigerator, covered, for up to 4 days.

CARAMELIZED WHITE CHOCOLATE ALMOND CUPCAKES

Sweet dreams are made of caramelized white chocolate! And they're even better if combined with almond! These super moist Almond Cupcakes are filled with Caramelized White Chocolate Ganache and topped with Caramelized White Chocolate Swiss Meringue Buttercream. If you have never tried caramelized white chocolate, this is your chance. It tastes like a mix between dulce de leche and white chocolate: silky, decadent and impossible to resist! These cupcakes will be love at first taste.

Makes 12 cupcakes

ALMOND CUPCAKES

1¼ cups (159 g) all-purpose flour

½ cup (48 g) almond flour

1¼ tsp (6 g) baking powder

½ tsp baking soda

½ tsp fine sea salt

½ cup (120 ml) vegetable oil

2 large eggs, at room temperature

¾ cup (150 g) granulated sugar

1 tsp vanilla extract

½ tsp almond extract

½ cup (120 ml) buttermilk,
at room temperature

CARAMELIZED WHITE CHOCOLATE GANACHE

1½ cups (255 g) chopped white chocolate (see Note on page 39)

¾ cup (180 ml) heavy cream

To make the Almond Cupcakes, preheat the oven to 350°F (177°C) and line 12 cupcake tins with cupcake liners.

In a large bowl, whisk together the all-purpose flour, almond flour, baking powder, baking soda and salt. Set aside.

In the bowl of an electric mixer, whisk together the oil and eggs until well combined. Add the granulated sugar and whisk for another minute, until smooth. Add the vanilla and almond extracts, followed by the buttermilk, and mix to combine. Lastly, add the dry ingredients and fold with a rubber spatula until incorporated.

Divide the batter evenly into the cupcake liners, filling them about two-thirds of the way. Bake for about 18 minutes. Start checking the cupcakes at the 15-minute mark, and keep baking and checking as necessary. To see if the cupcakes are ready, gently press with your finger on top of the cupcakes, and if they spring right back, that means they are done baking. Let the cupcakes cool completely before filling and frosting.

To make the Caramelized White Chocolate Ganache, preheat the oven to 215°F (102°C). Spread the chopped white chocolate on a rimmed baking sheet. Bake the chocolate for about 1 hour, stirring every 15 minutes with a spatula. Remove from the oven once the chocolate has a caramel color. Pour it into a bowl and stir to smooth it out.

Heat the heavy cream in a small saucepan or in the microwave until it is almost boiling, but don't let it come to a boil. Pour the heavy cream over the caramelized white chocolate. Stir with a whisk until incorporated. Set aside to cool completely to room temperature. Some will be used to make the frosting and some to fill the cupcakes.

(continued)

CARAMELIZED WHITE CHOCOLATE SWISS MERINGUE BUTTERCREAM

3 large egg whites

¾ cup (150 g) granulated sugar

1 cup plus 2 tbsp (255 g) unsalted butter, sliced into thin pieces, at room temperature

1⅓ cups (320 ml) Caramelized White Chocolate Ganache, plus more for filling

1 tsp vanilla extract

Blonde chocolate, chopped, for decorating (optional)

To make the Caramelized White Chocolate Swiss Meringue Buttercream, place the egg whites and granulated sugar in a bowl over a double boiler with barely simmering water. Make sure the bottom of the bowl isn't touching the water in the pan, so it doesn't cook the egg whites. Whisk the egg whites and sugar until the sugar melts and a candy thermometer reads 140°F (60°C). Remove the syrup from the heat.

With an electric mixer, beat the meringue with the whisk attachment, at high speed, until stiff peaks form. This might take 5 to 10 minutes, depending on your mixer. With my hand mixer, it takes me about 10 minutes, but it takes me about 5 minutes with my stand mixer. The meringue should be glossy and white.

Once the meringue has reached stiff peaks, start to add the butter, with the mixer on medium-high speed. Add one slab of butter at a time, waiting a few seconds before adding the next one. Keep whipping until the buttercream looks creamy and fluffy and all the butter has been incorporated. This can take anywhere from 5 to 10 minutes, depending on the temperature of the butter and how well the meringue has been whipped.

Once the buttercream looks fluffy and thick, add the 1⅓ cups (320 ml) of the cooled Caramelized White Chocolate Ganache, and whisk until incorporated. Finally, add the vanilla and mix to combine.

To assemble the cupcakes, use a spoon to remove the center of each cupcake. Spoon some of the remaining Caramelized White Chocolate Ganache into the middle of the cupcakes. Place the Caramelized White Chocolate Swiss Meringue Buttercream in a piping bag fitted with the piping tip of choice. Pipe the frosting over the cupcakes. Decorate the cupcakes with pieces of blonde chocolate, if desired.

Note: Use good-quality baking white chocolate, with at least 24% cocoa butter content. Don't use white chocolate chips or chocolate melts. If you are able to find caramelized white chocolate or blonde chocolate at a store, skip the caramelizing process, melt the same amount of blonde chocolate called for and skip to the buttercream step.

Cookie Monster

Cupcakes and cookies: The best of both worlds meet to bring you incredible cupcake recipes that are suitable for all cookie lovers *and* monsters! The cookie theme is explored throughout the following pages and takes all sorts of different shapes and textures in fun and innovative cupcakes!

From simple recipes, such as the Cookie Butter Cupcakes (page 43), to more elaborate and fancy ones, such as the Chocolate Marshmallow Cookie Cupcakes (page 47), you are sure to find a flavor combo that will suit your preferences. Or you can go for the decadent Marbled Banana Pudding Cupcakes (page 51), topped with a homemade vanilla wafer. The bottom line is, if you like cookies, and if you like cupcakes, then you have come to the right place!

COOKIE BUTTER CUPCAKES

Cookie butter has been all the rage lately, and for good reason. It's impossible to resist eating a spoonful as you open the jar to scoop some out to make these cupcakes, so I am going to suggest you buy a couple of jars for experimental purposes! This is one of the easiest cupcakes in the book, and it's up there with the most delicious ones too.

Makes 14 cupcakes

COOKIE BUTTER CUPCAKES

1¾ cups (221 g) all-purpose flour

1 tsp baking powder

¼ tsp baking soda

¼ tsp fine sea salt

¾ cup (169 g) unsalted butter, at room temperature

⅓ cup (82 g) cookie butter

¾ cup (150 g) granulated sugar

3 large eggs, at room temperature

1 tsp vanilla extract

⅓ cup (80 ml) buttermilk, at room temperature

COOKIE BUTTER BUTTERCREAM

¾ cup (169 g) unsalted butter, at room temperature

½ cup (125 g) cookie butter

2½ cups (300 g) powdered sugar, sifted

1 tsp vanilla extract

1 tsp milk, if needed

½ cup (125 g) cookie butter, for filling

To make the Cookie Butter Cupcakes, preheat the oven to 350°F (177°C) and line 14 cupcake tins with cupcake liners.

In a large bowl, sift together the flour, baking powder, baking soda and salt. Set aside.

In the bowl of an electric mixer, beat the butter on medium speed for about 45 seconds, until creamy. Add the cookie butter and mix until incorporated. Add the granulated sugar and beat for another minute. Scrape the sides of the bowl as necessary. Add the eggs, one at a time, mixing each egg until combined before adding the next. Add the vanilla and mix. Add the buttermilk and mix on low speed until combined. Finally, add the sifted dry ingredients and fold with a rubber spatula until incorporated.

Divide the batter evenly into the cupcake liners, filling them about two-thirds of the way. Bake for about 18 minutes. Start checking the cupcakes at the 15-minute mark, and keep baking and checking as necessary. To see if the cupcakes are ready, gently press with your finger on top of the cupcakes, and if they spring right back, that means they are done baking. Let the cupcakes cool completely before filling and frosting.

To make the Cookie Butter Buttercream, place the butter in a bowl and cream with an electric mixer for 4 minutes on medium-high speed. Add the cookie butter and cream with the butter for another minute. Meanwhile, add the sifted powdered sugar to the bowl. Mix on low speed until the mixture is incorporated and you see no more streaks of dry powdered sugar. Increase the speed to medium-high, and beat for another minute. Add the vanilla and mix until combined. If the buttercream seems too stiff, add the milk until you have achieved the perfect consistency. If the buttercream is too runny, add more powdered sugar as necessary.

To assemble the cupcakes, use a spoon to remove the center of each cupcake. Spoon about 2 teaspoons (10 g) of cookie butter into the middle of the cupcakes. Place the Cookie Butter Buttercream in a piping bag fitted with the piping tip of choice. Pipe the frosting over the cupcakes.

PRETZEL CHOCOLATE CHIP COOKIE DOUGH CUPCAKES

Picture this: a fluffy Vanilla Cupcake, brimming with chocolate chips, filled with creamy Edible Cookie Dough, topped with a decadent Brown Sugar Frosting, and a Pretzel Chocolate Chip Cookie to finish in style. This is the kind of cupcake that will turn heads and make mouths water!

Makes 14 cupcakes

VANILLA CUPCAKES

1½ cups (191 g) all-purpose flour

1 tsp baking powder

¼ tsp baking soda

¼ tsp fine sea salt

½ cup (113 g) unsalted butter, at room temperature

1 cup (200 g) granulated sugar

3 large eggs, at room temperature

1 tsp vanilla extract

½ cup (120 ml) milk, at room temperature

½ cup (85 g) semisweet chocolate chips

EDIBLE COOKIE DOUGH

¼ cup (31 g) all-purpose flour

2 tbsp (28 g) unsalted butter, at room temperature

2½ tbsp (31 g) packed brown sugar

⅛ tsp fine sea salt

2 tsp (10 ml) milk

¼ tsp vanilla extract

2 tbsp (21 g) mini semisweet chocolate chips

To make the Vanilla Cupcakes, preheat the oven to 350°F (177°C) and line 14 cupcake tins with cupcake liners.

In a large bowl, sift together the flour, baking powder, baking soda and salt. Set aside. In the bowl of an electric mixer, beat the butter on medium speed for about 1 minute. Add the granulated sugar and beat for another 1 to 2 minutes, until creamy and fluffy. Scrape the sides of the bowl as necessary.

Add the eggs, one at a time, mixing each egg until combined before adding the next. Add the vanilla, followed by the milk, and mix to combine. Add the dry ingredients and fold with a rubber spatula until incorporated. Last, but not least, add the chocolate chips and mix briefly just until incorporated, about 20 seconds.

Divide the batter evenly into the cupcake liners, filling them about two-thirds of the way. Bake for about 18 minutes. Start checking the cupcakes at the 15-minute mark, and keep baking and checking as necessary. To see if the cupcakes are ready, gently press with your finger on top of the cupcakes, and if they spring right back, that means they are done baking. Let the cupcakes cool completely before filling and frosting.

To make the Edible Cookie Dough, begin by heat-treating the flour to kill any bacteria and make it safe for raw consumption. Preheat the oven to 350°F (177°C) and line a baking sheet with parchment paper. Evenly spread the flour on the prepared baking sheet. Place it in the oven and bake for 3 minutes, or until it registers 160°F (71°C) on an instant-read thermometer. Cool completely before using. Also please note that, if doubling this recipe and baking more flour, the baking time should be extended by a few minutes but no more than 5 minutes.

After treating the flour and cooling it down, place the butter in a bowl and cream with an electric mixer for 2 minutes. Add the brown sugar and beat for another 2 minutes, until the mixture is lightened in color and fluffy. With the mixer off, add the flour and salt and then mix until combined. Add the milk and vanilla and stir briefly. Finally, add the chocolate chips and fold with a rubber spatula until incorporated. Keep the cookie dough covered until ready to use.

(continued)

COOKIE DOUGH CUPCAKES

Have you ever started making chocolate chip cookies and found yourself wanting to eat the whole bowl of cookie dough before even baking the cookies? Well, these Cookie Dough Cupcakes are here to make those dreams come true! They are one of the easiest cupcakes in the whole book to make. Each of these Vanilla Cupcakes is filled and then topped with a proper amount of Edible Cookie Dough that will satisfy your most indulgent cravings! They are just like eating a whole bowl of chocolate chip cookie dough, but in cupcake form, which you have to agree with me, is way better!

Makes 14 cupcakes

VANILLA CUPCAKES

1½ cups (191 g) all-purpose flour

1 tsp baking powder

¼ tsp baking soda

¼ tsp fine sea salt

½ cup (113 g) unsalted butter, at room temperature

1 cup (200 g) granulated sugar

3 large eggs, at room temperature

1 tsp vanilla extract

½ cup (120 ml) milk, at room temperature

½ cup (85 g) semisweet chocolate chips

To make the Vanilla Cupcakes, preheat the oven to 350°F (177°C) and line 14 cupcake tins with cupcake liners.

In a large bowl, sift together the flour, baking powder, baking soda and salt. Set aside.

In the bowl of an electric mixer, beat the butter on medium speed for about 1 minute. Add the granulated sugar and beat for another 1 to 2 minutes, until creamy and fluffy. Scrape the sides of the bowl as necessary.

Add the eggs, one at a time, mixing each egg until combined before adding the next. Add the vanilla, followed by the milk, and mix to combine. Add the dry ingredients and fold with a rubber spatula until incorporated. Last, but not least, add the chocolate chips and mix briefly.

Divide the batter evenly into the cupcake liners, filling them about two-thirds of the way. Bake for about 18 minutes. Start checking the cupcakes at the 15-minute mark, and keep baking and checking as necessary. To see if the cupcakes are ready, gently press with your finger on top of the cupcakes, and if they spring right back, that means they are done baking. Let the cupcakes cool completely before filling and frosting.

(continued)

EDIBLE COOKIE DOUGH

2½ cups (318 g) all-purpose flour

1¼ cups (282 g) unsalted butter, at room temperature

1½ cups (300 g) packed brown sugar

½ tsp fine sea salt

¼ cup (60 ml) milk

1½ tsp (7 ml) vanilla extract

1¼ cups (212 g) semisweet chocolate chips

To make the Edible Cookie Dough, begin by heat-treating the flour to kill any bacteria and make it safe for raw consumption. Preheat the oven to 350°F (177°C) and line a baking sheet with parchment paper. Evenly spread the flour on the prepared baking sheet. Place it in the oven and bake for 5 to 7 minutes, or until it registers 160°F (71°C) on an instant-read thermometer. Cool completely before using.

After treating the flour and cooling it down, place the butter in a bowl and cream with an electric mixer for 3 minutes. Add the brown sugar and beat for another 4 minutes, until the mixture is lightened in color and fluffy. With the mixer off, add the flour and salt, then mix until combined. Add the milk and vanilla and stir briefly. Finally, add the chocolate chips and fold with a rubber spatula until incorporated. Keep the cookie dough covered until ready to use.

To assemble the cupcakes, use a spoon to remove the center of each cupcake. Spoon the Edible Cookie Dough into the middle of each cupcake. I used a large ice cream scoop to scoop out the dough to top the cupcakes, and gently shaped them into a ball with my hands.

The cupcakes can be stored in the refrigerator, covered, for up to 4 days. Let them come to room temperature slightly before serving.

Fudge IT Up!

The cupcakes you will see on the next pages are filled with fudgy goodness! Fudge makes for such a fabulous cupcake filling, because there's nothing like biting into a fluffy cupcake and getting a mouthful of velvety and creamy fudge!

Some of my most beloved cupcakes from the whole book live in this chapter, such as the Salted Tahini Cupcakes (page 61), filled with a rich tahini fudge, and the Chocolate Fudge Carrot Cupcakes (page 73), which are unlike any carrot cake you've ever had before. They are made the Brazilian way and are filled and topped with a scrumptious and gooey chocolate fudge.

The highlight of the chapter is probably the White Chocolate Macadamia and Caramel Fudge Cupcakes (page 74), because they are topped with a delicious White Chocolate Macadamia and Caramel Cluster, like the ones you get at those old-fashioned fudge shoppes. You will feel like a confectionist extraordinaire!

SALTED TAHINI CUPCAKES

This recipe is on the list of my favorites from the book! The tahini taste really shines in these cupcakes. While the tahini is more of a supporting element in the other tahini cupcake in this book (Tahini Caramel Banana Cupcakes, page 81), here it is the star of the show! You will taste the exquisite sweet and savory flavor profile through every bite of these cupcakes. The cupcakes themselves have tahini in the batter, which adds a bit of a nutty taste, and they are filled with the most luscious Tahini Fudge, which I almost ate in full before I could even proceed with assembling the cupcakes. On top of the cupcakes, Salted Tahini Buttercream cuts through the sweetness of the filling, enhancing the tahini qualities even more!

Makes 14 cupcakes

TAHINI CUPCAKES

1½ cups (191 g) all-purpose flour

1 tsp baking powder

¼ tsp baking soda

¼ tsp fine sea salt

½ cup (113 g) unsalted butter, at room temperature

1 cup (200 g) granulated sugar

¼ cup (60 ml) tahini

2 large eggs, at room temperature

1 tsp vanilla extract

½ cup (120 ml) buttermilk, at room temperature

TAHINI FUDGE

⅔ cup (156 ml) condensed milk

⅓ cup (78 ml) tahini

½ tbsp (7 g) unsalted butter

To make the Tahini Cupcakes, preheat the oven to 350°F (177°C) and line 14 cupcake tins with cupcake liners.

In a large bowl, sift together the flour, baking powder, baking soda and salt. Set aside. In the bowl of an electric mixer, beat the butter on medium speed for about 1 minute. Add the granulated sugar and beat for another 1 to 2 minutes, until creamy and fluffy. Scrape the sides of the bowl as necessary. Add the tahini and blend again.

Add the eggs, one at a time, mixing each egg until combined before adding the next. Add the vanilla, followed by the buttermilk, and blend again. Lastly, add the dry ingredients and fold with a rubber spatula until incorporated.

Divide the batter evenly into the cupcake liners, filling them about two-thirds of the way. Bake for about 18 minutes. Start checking the cupcakes at the 15-minute mark, and keep baking and checking as necessary. To see if the cupcakes are ready, gently press with your finger on top of the cupcakes, and if they spring right back, that means they are done baking. Let the cupcakes cool completely before filling and frosting.

To make the Tahini Fudge, place the condensed milk, tahini and butter in a small saucepan over medium heat and cook for 12 to 15 minutes, stirring nonstop. If you stop stirring, the fudge will stick to the bottom of the pan. Cook until the mixture is thick and fudgy and you can see the bottom of the pan when you run the spatula through the middle of the fudge.

Remove to a small bowl and let it cool completely. Don't place it in the fridge before filling the cupcakes or the fudge will get too hard to be piped or spooned into the cupcakes. It can be kept covered, at room temperature, for up to 1 day.

(continued)

SALTED TAHINI BUTTERCREAM

1½ cups (339 g) unsalted butter, at room temperature

½ cup (120 g) tahini

3 cups (382 g) powdered sugar, sifted

1½ tsp (7 ml) vanilla extract

2 tbsp (30 ml) milk

½ tsp salt, or to taste

To make the Salted Tahini Buttercream, place the butter in the bowl of an electric mixer. Cream on medium-high speed for about 4 minutes, until very fluffy and lightened in color. Add the tahini and mix until combined.

With the mixer off, add the sifted powdered sugar to the bowl. Mix on low speed until the sugar has incorporated with the butter. Increase the speed to medium-high and beat the butter and sugar together for about 1 minute, until creamy and fluffy. Add the vanilla and milk, and mix until combined. Add the salt to taste, starting with ½ teaspoon, and if you feel like you want it a bit saltier, add more as desired.

If the buttercream is too runny, add more sifted powdered sugar by the tablespoon (8 g) and mix to incorporate. If the buttercream is too stiff, add a bit more milk by the teaspoon, mixing in between, until you achieve a buttercream that is creamy, firm and smooth.

To assemble the cupcakes, use a spoon to remove the center of each cupcake. Spoon or pipe some of the Tahini Fudge into the middle of the cupcakes. Place the Salted Tahini Buttercream in a piping bag fitted with the piping tip of choice. Pipe the frosting over the cupcakes.

The cupcakes can be stored in the refrigerator, covered, for up to 4 days.

CHOCOLATE PEANUT BUTTER CUPCAKES

What could be better than the classic chocolate and peanut butter combo? Oh, I know! If there's fudge involved! These cupcakes are filled and topped with Peanut Butter Fudge, adding a layer of sticky goodness to each bite. The fudge element is an exciting addition to this traditional flavor combo. You bite into a fluffy chocolate cupcake and get a mouthful of the gooey fudge, and the silky Chocolate Peanut Butter Buttercream makes these cupcakes intensely decadent and delicious.

Makes 14 cupcakes

CHOCOLATE CUPCAKES

1½ cups (190 g) all-purpose flour

¼ cup (31 g) unsweetened cocoa powder

1 tsp espresso powder (optional)

1 tsp baking soda

¾ tsp baking powder

½ tsp fine sea salt

½ cup (120 ml) canola oil

1 cup (200 g) granulated sugar

1 cup (240 ml) brewed coffee or hot water

1 tbsp (15 ml) white vinegar

2 tsp (10 ml) vanilla extract

PEANUT BUTTER FUDGE

2 (14-oz [397-g]) cans condensed milk

¼ cup (62 g) creamy peanut butter

3 tbsp (42 g) unsalted butter, divided

½ cup (75 g) chopped peanuts

To make the Chocolate Cupcakes, preheat the oven to 350°F (177°C) and line 14 cupcake tins with cupcake liners.

In a large bowl, sift together the flour, cocoa powder, espresso powder (if using), baking soda, baking powder and salt; set aside. In another bowl, mix the oil, granulated sugar, coffee, vinegar and vanilla. Pour the dry mixture over the wet ingredients and whisk briefly, until incorporated. Be careful not to overmix. As soon as you see no more streaks of dry mixture, stop whisking.

Divide the batter evenly among the cupcake liners, filling them about two-thirds of the way. Bake the cupcakes for about 18 minutes. Start checking the cupcakes at the 15-minute mark, and keep baking and checking as necessary. To see if the cupcakes are ready, gently press with your finger on top of the cupcakes, and if they spring right back, that means they are done baking. Let the cupcakes cool completely before filling and frosting.

To make the Peanut Butter Fudge, place the condensed milk, peanut butter and 2 tablespoons (28 g) of the butter in a small saucepan. Cook over medium heat for 12 to 15 minutes, stirring nonstop. If you stop stirring, the fudge will stick to the bottom of the pan. Cook until the mixture is thick and fudgy and you can see the bottom of the pan when you run the spatula through the middle of the fudge.

Remove to a small bowl and let it cool completely. Don't place it in the fridge before filling or the fudge will get too hard to be piped or spooned into the cupcakes. The fudge can be kept covered, at room temperature, for up to 1 day. Reserve about ⅔ cup (196 g) of the fudge to fill the cupcakes, and the rest you can roll into truffles to decorate the top of the cupcakes.

(continued)

CHOCOLATE FUDGE CARROT CUPCAKES

Have you ever tried carrot cake with chocolate instead of cream cheese frosting? Hear me out on this one! This is how we make carrot cake in Brazil, by topping it with chocolate frosting, or with *brigadeiro*, which is a chocolate fudge made with condensed milk. Unlike its American counterpart, this version of Carrot Cupcakes doesn't take any cinnamon or spices. The flavor of the carrot shines through the super moist cake, complemented by the rich and delicious Chocolate Fudge. This is probably my favorite cupcake of the whole chapter.

Makes 12 cupcakes

CARROT CUPCAKES

1½ cups (191 g) all-purpose flour

1 tsp baking powder

¼ tsp baking soda

¼ tsp fine sea salt

1 ⅔ cups (200 g) chopped carrots

½ cup (120 ml) vegetable oil

2 large eggs, at room temperature

1 tsp vanilla extract

¼ cup (60 ml) milk, at room temperature

CHOCOLATE FUDGE

2 (14-oz [397-g]) cans condensed milk

2 tbsp (28 g) unsalted butter

½ cup (85 g) semisweet chopped chocolate or chocolate chips

To make the Carrot Cupcakes, preheat the oven to 350°F (177°C) and line 12 cupcake tins with cupcake liners.

In a large bowl, sift together the flour, baking powder, baking soda and salt. Set aside.

Place the chopped carrots and oil in a blender and blend for 1 to 2 minutes, until the carrots are pureed and you no longer see chunks of carrots in the mixture. Add the eggs, vanilla and milk to the blender. Blend the mixture for about 20 seconds, until completely incorporated and smooth. Pour the blended ingredients into a bowl and add the sifted dry ingredients. Gently mix with a whisk until the batter is incorporated.

Divide the batter among the cupcake liners, filling them about two-thirds of the way. Bake for 18 to 20 minutes. To see if the cupcakes are ready, gently press with your finger on top of the cupcakes, and if they spring right back, that means they are done baking. Let the cupcakes cool completely before filling and frosting.

To make the Chocolate Fudge, place the condensed milk, butter and chocolate in a small saucepan. Cook over medium heat for 12 to 15 minutes, stirring nonstop. If you stop stirring, the fudge will stick to the bottom of the pan. Cook until the mixture is thick and fudgy and you can see the bottom of the pan when you run the spatula through the middle of the fudge. Remove to a small bowl and let it cool completely. Don't place it in the fridge before filling and frosting the cupcakes, or the fudge will get too hard to be piped. The fudge can be kept at room temperature, covered, for up to 1 day.

To assemble the cupcakes, remove the center of each cupcake with a spoon. Place the cooled fudge filling in a piping bag fitted with the tip of choice. Pipe some filling into the middle of each cupcake and continue piping all the way to the top to frost the cupcakes.

The cupcakes can be stored in the refrigerator, covered, for up to 4 days, if you can go that long without eating them all!

WHITE CHOCOLATE MACADAMIA AND CARAMEL FUDGE CUPCAKES

The idea for these cupcakes came when I had a white chocolate macadamia cluster candy from a local bakery. I thought it was the best treat in the world. The combination of the gooey caramel and the naturally buttery macadamia nuts, wrapped in rich white chocolate, blew my mind, and I just had to replicate it. But not only that, I also had to turn it into a cupcake somehow! So here I present to you the best treat in the world, in cupcake form! Vanilla Cupcakes feature a luscious and gooey Caramel and Macadamia Fudge Filling, are topped with a velvety White Chocolate Buttercream, and sport a White Chocolate Macadamia and Caramel Cluster candy, just like the one that prompted the idea of this cupcake in the first place.

Makes 14 cupcakes

VANILLA CUPCAKES

1½ cups (191 g) all-purpose flour

1 tsp baking powder

¼ tsp baking soda

¼ tsp fine sea salt

½ cup (113 g) unsalted butter, at room temperature

1 cup (200 g) granulated sugar

3 large eggs, at room temperature

1 tsp vanilla extract

½ cup (120 ml) milk, at room temperature

To make the Vanilla Cupcakes, preheat the oven to 350°F (177°C) and line 14 cupcake tins with cupcake liners.

In a large bowl, sift together the flour, baking powder, baking soda and salt. Set aside.

In the bowl of an electric mixer, beat the butter on medium speed for about 1 minute. Add the granulated sugar and beat for another 1 to 2 minutes, until creamy and fluffy. Scrape the sides of the bowl as necessary.

Add the eggs, one at a time, mixing each egg until combined before adding the next. Add the vanilla, followed by the milk, and mix to combine. Lastly, add the dry ingredients and fold with a rubber spatula until incorporated.

Divide the batter evenly among the cupcake liners, filling them about two-thirds of the way. Bake for about 18 minutes. Start checking the cupcakes at the 15-minute mark, and keep baking and checking as necessary. To see if the cupcakes are ready, gently press with your finger on top of the cupcakes, and if they spring right back, that means they are done baking. Let the cupcakes cool completely before filling and frosting.

(continued)

CARAMEL AND MACADAMIA FUDGE FILLING

¼ cup (38 g) macadamia nuts

⅔ cup (156 ml) condensed milk

½ cup (70 g) unwrapped soft caramel candies

½ tbsp (7 g) unsalted butter

WHITE CHOCOLATE MACADAMIA AND CARAMEL CLUSTERS

⅔ cup (91 g) macadamia nuts

¾ cup (105 g) unwrapped soft caramel candies

2 tsp (10 ml) heavy cream

⅔ cup (113 g) white chocolate, chopped

To make the Caramel and Macadamia Fudge Filling, place the macadamia nuts in a small food processor and process until they are finely crushed.

In a small saucepan, combine the crushed macadamias, condensed milk, caramel candies and butter. Cook over medium heat for 12 to 15 minutes, stirring nonstop. If you stop stirring, the fudge will stick to the bottom of the pan. Cook until the mixture is thick and fudgy and you can see the bottom of the pan when you run the spatula through the middle of the fudge.

Remove to a small bowl and let it cool completely. Don't place it in the fridge before filling the cupcakes, or the fudge will get too hard to be piped. It can be kept at room temperature, covered, for up to 1 day.

To make the White Chocolate Macadamia and Caramel Clusters, line a baking sheet with parchment paper. Create about 18 clusters with 4 or 5 macadamias each on the prepared baking sheet. The amount of macadamias per cluster will depend on the size of the macadamias you are using and whether they are halved or whole. I used halved macadamias, and most clusters had 4 macadamias, but some clusters had 5 because the macadamias were smaller. You can also use a mini cupcake silicone pan to do this, because it will perfectly fit 4 or 5 macadamias in each cup, and the silicone will make it easy to remove the candies later.

Place the caramel candies and heavy cream in a microwave-safe bowl. Microwave in 15-second intervals, stirring in between, until the caramel is entirely melted and incorporated with the cream. Use a spoon to pour small amounts of caramel over the clusters of macadamias, distributing it evenly among all the nuts. Let it set for a few minutes.

In a microwave-safe bowl, melt the white chocolate in the microwave in 15-second intervals, stirring in between, until completely melted and smooth. Pour the white chocolate over the candies, distributing it evenly among all clusters. You can use a spoon to do this, or place the chocolate in a piping bag and pipe it over the macadamias.

Let the candies sit until the chocolate and the caramel are set and dry. You can place them in the fridge to speed this up.

WHITE CHOCOLATE BUTTERCREAM

1 cup plus 1 tbsp (200 g) white chocolate, chopped

1 cup (226 g) unsalted butter, at room temperature

2 cups (250 g) powdered sugar, sifted

To make the White Chocolate Buttercream, in a microwave-safe bowl, melt the white chocolate in the microwave in 15-second intervals, stirring in between, until completely melted and smooth. Let cool.

While the chocolate cools, in a separate bowl, beat the butter with an electric mixer on medium-high speed for 4 minutes, until fluffy and lightened in color. Turn the mixer off, add the sifted powdered sugar and mix on low speed to combine. Increase the speed to medium and beat the mixture for 1 more minute. Add the melted and cooled white chocolate and mix until incorporated, scraping the sides of the bowl if necessary. Note that the chocolate must be cooled down, not hot, but also not cold or hardened. If the chocolate is hot or warm, it will melt the butter, and if it's cold or starting to get hard, it will form lumps in the buttercream.

If the buttercream seems runny, add more sifted powdered sugar until you achieve the desired consistency. If the buttercream seems stiff, add milk, 1 teaspoon at a time, stirring in between, until you achieve the perfect consistency. Keep the buttercream covered until you are ready to frost the cupcakes.

To assemble the cupcakes, use a spoon to remove the center of each cupcake. Place the Caramel and Macadamia Fudge Filling in a piping bag and pipe it into the middle of the cupcakes. Place the White Chocolate Buttercream in a piping bag fitted with the tip of choice, and pipe the frosting on top of the cupcakes. Top each cupcake with a White Chocolate Macadamia and Caramel Cluster.

The cupcakes can be stored in the refrigerator, covered, for up to 4 days. Let them come to room temperature slightly before serving so the fudge and the candy on top have a chance to soften up a bit.

Caramel Lovers

Delightfully sticky, sinfully gooey, caramel is the star of this chapter, where I offer you a collection of the most delectable caramel cupcake recipes. In drizzles, layers or fillings, caramel is beloved by all because it brings depth, richness and a silky element to whatever dessert it is added to.

One of my main flavors to pair with caramel is banana, like in the Tahini Caramel Banana Cupcakes (page 81), which features a velvety tahini caramel sauce. And caramel can also be good on its own, especially if we are talking about dulce de leche, as you will find out when you make the Salted Dulce de Leche Cupcakes (page 95). If you are looking for a super-rich cupcake flavor, go with the Chocolate Turtle Cupcakes (page 87), where caramel joins forces with chocolate and pecans to form an exceptional treat that will set the bar high for any other caramel cupcake you ever try after this!

TAHINI CARAMEL BANANA CUPCAKES

Have you tried baking with tahini yet? If you haven't, get in that kitchen ASAP! Tahini is nutty, slightly sweet and super creamy, and has just a tad of bitterness to it, which makes it perfect for desserts! In these cupcakes, tahini is made into silky caramel, which is then used to fill fluffy Banana Cupcakes and to make a scrumptious, light and fluffy Tahini Caramel Swiss Meringue Buttercream.

Makes 12 cupcakes

BANANA CUPCAKES

1½ cups (191 g) all-purpose flour

1½ tsp (7 g) baking powder

¼ tsp baking soda

¼ tsp fine sea salt

½ cup (120 ml) vegetable oil

¾ cup (150 g) granulated sugar

2 large eggs

1 tsp vanilla extract

⅔ cup (146 g) mashed banana

TAHINI CARAMEL SAUCE

1 cup (200 g) granulated sugar

¼ cup (60 ml) water

¼ cup (60 g) tahini

2 tbsp (28 g) unsalted butter

⅔ cup (158 ml) heavy cream

To make the Banana Cupcakes, preheat the oven to 350°F (177°C) and line 12 cupcake tins with cupcake liners.

In a large bowl, sift together the flour, baking powder, baking soda and salt. Set aside. In a separate large bowl, whisk the oil with the granulated sugar for 1 minute, until incorporated. Add the eggs, one at a time, mixing each egg fully before adding the next. Add the vanilla and mashed banana and stir. Lastly, add the dry ingredients and fold with a rubber spatula until incorporated.

Divide the batter evenly among the cupcake liners, filling them about two-thirds of the way. Bake for about 18 minutes. Start checking the cupcakes at the 15-minute mark, and keep baking and checking as necessary. To see if the cupcakes are ready, gently press with your finger on top of the cupcakes, and if they spring right back, that means they are done baking. Let the cupcakes cool completely before filling and frosting.

To make the Tahini Caramel Sauce, place the granulated sugar and water in a small saucepan over medium heat. Use a spatula to stir the sugar until it melts completely. Don't stop stirring; it's important to make sure the sugar is melting evenly. Keep cooking the sugar and water syrup until it starts caramelizing; don't stir with a spatula at this point, simply swirl the pan around to distribute the heat evenly. The syrup will start to have an amber color after about 7 minutes.

As soon as the syrup has a deep amber color, remove the pan from the heat and carefully add the tahini and butter. Stir until the butter melts, then add the heavy cream. Be careful with this step, as the caramel will bubble up. Return the pan to the heat and cook the caramel for 30 seconds over low heat, just to bring the ingredients together. You are just looking to incorporate the sugar syrup with the butter and heavy cream. If you cook too long, the caramel will become hard as it cools.

(continued)

TAHINI CARAMEL SWISS MERINGUE BUTTERCREAM

3 large egg whites

¾ cup (150 g) granulated sugar

15 tbsp (210 g) unsalted butter, sliced into thin pieces, at room temperature

⅓ cup (78 ml) Tahini Caramel Sauce

¼ tsp vanilla extract

Remove the caramel from the heat and pour it into a bowl. Let it come to room temperature before filling the cupcakes. If you make the caramel ahead, store it in the fridge and then reheat it gently for a few seconds in the microwave before filling the cupcakes.

To make the Tahini Caramel Swiss Meringue Buttercream, mix the egg whites and granulated sugar in a heatproof bowl. Place the bowl over a small pan with barely simmering water to form a double boiler. Make sure the bottom of the bowl isn't in contact with the water in the pan. Whisk the sugar and egg whites until they reach 140°F (60°C) on a candy thermometer, then remove from the heat.

In an electric mixer, beat the egg white mixture with the whisk attachment at high speed, until stiff peaks form. This might take from 5 to 10 minutes, depending on your mixer. With my hand mixer, it takes me about 10 minutes, but it takes me about 5 minutes with my stand mixer. The meringue should be glossy and white.

Now start to add the butter, with the mixer on medium-high speed. Add one slab of butter at a time, waiting a few seconds before adding the next one. Keep whipping until the buttercream looks creamy and fluffy and all the butter has been incorporated. This can take anywhere from 5 to 10 minutes, depending on the temperature of the butter and how well the meringue has been whipped. Once the buttercream has come together and is fluffy and creamy, add the cooled Tahini Caramel Sauce and mix until incorporated. Lastly, add the vanilla and mix.

To assemble the cupcakes, remove the center of each cupcake with a spoon. Next, spoon some of the Tahini Caramel Sauce into the middle of each cupcake. Place the Tahini Caramel Swiss Meringue Buttercream in a large piping bag fitted with the tip of choice. Pipe the frosting on top of the cupcakes.

The cupcakes can be stored in the refrigerator, covered, for up to 4 days. Let the cupcakes come to room temperature slightly before serving, so the caramel has a chance to soften up a bit.

Troubleshooting Tips: If the buttercream is looking soupy, or doesn't seem to become fluffy and creamy, it might be for a couple of reasons. Number one: You didn't whip the meringue until stiff peaks were formed, and in this case, it will be very hard to get this buttercream to work and you mostly likely have to start over. Or it might be that your kitchen is too hot or the butter was too soft when you started to add it. In this case, you can try placing the bowl of the mixer in the freezer for about 5 minutes, then continue whipping, and your meringue will most likely start to get creamy and fluffy.

DULCE DE LECHE COCONUT CUPCAKES

In these splendid cupcakes, some of the best flavors in the world come together in a heavenly balance of textures and taste. The light and fluffy Coconut Swiss Meringue Buttercream is the ideal complement to the Chocolate Coconut Cupcakes and Dulce de Leche Coconut Filling. Toasted coconut flakes make the perfect garnish.

Makes 14 cupcakes

CHOCOLATE COCONUT CUPCAKES

1 cup (127 g) all-purpose flour

⅓ cup (41 g) unsweetened cocoa powder

1 tsp baking powder

¾ tsp baking soda

¼ tsp fine sea salt

⅓ cup (78 ml) vegetable oil

1 cup (200 g) granulated sugar

½ cup (120 ml) coconut milk

1 large egg, at room temperature

1 tsp vanilla extract

½ cup (120 ml) hot brewed coffee or hot water

DULCE DE LECHE COCONUT FILLING

¾ cup (180 ml) condensed milk

½ cup (47 g) sweetened shredded coconut

To make the Chocolate Coconut Cupcakes, preheat the oven to 350°F (177°C) and line 14 cupcake tins with cupcake liners.

In a large bowl, sift together the flour, cocoa powder, baking powder, baking soda and salt; set aside.

In another bowl, whisk together the oil, granulated sugar, coconut milk, egg and vanilla until the mixture is smooth. Add the dry mixture to the wet ingredients and whisk briefly, until incorporated. Be careful not to overmix. As soon as you see no more streaks of dry mixture, stop whisking. Add the hot coffee, and whisk until incorporated. The batter will be thin.

Divide the batter evenly among the cupcake liners, filling them about two-thirds of the way. Bake the cupcakes for about 18 minutes. Start checking the cupcakes at the 15-minute mark, and keep baking and checking as necessary. To see if the cupcakes are ready, gently press with your finger on top of the cupcakes, and if they spring right back, that means they are done baking. Let the cupcakes cool completely before filling and frosting.

To make the Dulce de Leche Coconut Filling, preheat the oven to 350°F (177°C).

Pour the condensed milk into a small oven-proof bowl and cover it with foil. Place the bowl in a larger oven-proof pan, and fill the large pan with water to create a water bath. Bake the condensed milk in the oven for 2 to 3 hours, stirring every hour.

Once the condensed milk has a deep caramel color and is thick, remove it from the oven. Let it cool completely, and preferably refrigerate it for a few hours before using it. Before using it to fill the cupcakes, stir in the shredded coconut.

(continued)

COCONUT SWISS MERINGUE BUTTERCREAM

3 large egg whites

1 cup (200 g) granulated sugar

18 tbsp (255 g) unsalted butter, sliced into thin pieces, at room temperature

1 tsp coconut extract

¼ cup (23 g) shredded coconut

To make the Coconut Swiss Meringue Buttercream, mix the egg whites and granulated sugar in a heatproof bowl. Place the bowl over a small pan with barely simmering water to form a double boiler. Make sure the bottom of the bowl isn't in contact with the water in the pan, because you don't want the egg whites to cook in the double boiler. Whisk the sugar and egg whites until they reach 140°F (60°C) on a candy thermometer, then remove from the heat.

In an electric mixer, beat the egg white mixture with the whisk attachment at high speed, until stiff peaks form. This might take from 5 to 10 minutes, depending on your mixer. With my hand mixer, it takes me about 10 minutes, but it takes me about 5 minutes in my stand mixer. The meringue should be glossy and white.

Now start to add the butter, with the mixer on medium-high speed. Add one slab of butter at a time, waiting a few seconds before adding the next one. Keep whipping until the buttercream looks creamy and fluffy and all the butter has been incorporated. This can take anywhere from 5 to 10 minutes, depending on the temperature of the butter and how well the meringue has been whipped. Lastly, add the coconut extract.

Spread the shredded coconut in a nonstick pan over medium heat and toast, stirring the coconut flakes constantly, as they start to brown. Keep your eye on the coconut flakes as you cook them, because they tend to brown very fast. Once they are slightly browned, remove them from the heat and let them cool before sprinkling over the cupcakes.

To assemble the cupcakes, use a spoon to remove the center of each cupcake. Spoon some of the Dulce de Leche Coconut Filling into the middle of the cupcakes. Place the Coconut Swiss Meringue Buttercream in a piping bag fitted with the piping tip of choice. Pipe the frosting over the cupcakes. Sprinkle each cupcake with some toasted coconut flakes.

The cupcakes can be stored in the refrigerator, covered, for up to 4 days.

Note: You can make the dulce de leche yourself following the recipe, or you can use store-bought dulce de leche.

CHOCOLATE TURTLE CUPCAKES

This delightful confection features fluffy Chocolate Cupcakes, with a velvety and nutty Pecan Caramel Filling, topped with a bold and intense Chocolate Cream Cheese Frosting. And to decorate each cupcake there's a buttery Turtle Candy, which is a treat in and of itself. Possibly one of the most over-the-top cupcakes ever! This is the cupcake you make when you want to enchant your guests.

Makes 14 cupcakes

CHOCOLATE CUPCAKES

1½ cups (190 g) all-purpose flour

¼ cup (31 g) unsweetened cocoa powder

1 tsp espresso powder (optional)

1 tsp baking soda

¾ tsp baking powder

½ tsp fine sea salt

½ cup (120 ml) canola oil

1 cup (200 g) granulated sugar

1 cup (240 ml) brewed coffee or hot water

1 tbsp (15 ml) white vinegar

2 tsp (10 ml) vanilla extract

PECAN CARAMEL FILLING

½ cup (52 g) toasted pecans

1¼ cups (170 g) unwrapped soft caramel candies

¼ cup (60 ml) heavy cream

To make the Chocolate Cupcakes, preheat the oven to 350°F (177°C) and line 14 cupcake tins with cupcake liners.

In a large bowl, sift together the flour, cocoa powder, espresso powder (if using), baking soda, baking powder and salt; set aside.

In another bowl, mix together the oil, granulated sugar, coffee, vinegar and vanilla. Pour the dry mixture over the wet ingredients and whisk briefly, until incorporated. Be careful not to overmix. As soon as you see no more streaks of dry mixture, stop whisking.

Divide the batter evenly among the cupcake liners, filling them about two-thirds of the way. Bake the cupcakes for about 18 minutes. Start checking the cupcakes at the 15-minute mark, and keep baking and checking as necessary. To see if the cupcakes are ready, gently press with your finger on top of the cupcakes, and if they spring right back, that means they are done baking. Let the cupcakes cool completely before filling and frosting.

To make the Pecan Caramel Filling, place the pecans in a small food processor and pulse until they are finely ground.

Combine the unwrapped caramels and the heavy cream in a small saucepan over medium heat, and stir constantly while the mixture heats up. Keep cooking the mixture slowly until the caramel has entirely melted and combined with the heavy cream. Add the finely ground pecans and stir to combine. Don't let the mixture come to a boil. Remove from the heat, pour into a bowl and set aside to cool to room temperature.

(continued)

CHOCOLATE CREAM CHEESE FROSTING

⅔ cup (113 g) chopped dark chocolate

2¼ cups (281 g) powdered sugar

⅔ cup (74 g) cocoa powder

1 cup (226 g) cream cheese, at room temperature

6 tbsp (84 g) unsalted butter, at room temperature

1 tsp vanilla extract

2 tbsp (30 ml) heavy cream, if needed

TURTLE CANDY

1¼ cups (130 g) toasted pecans

1¼ cups (170 g) unwrapped soft caramel candies

1½ tsp (7 ml) heavy cream

⅔ cup (113 g) semisweet chopped chocolate or chocolate chips

½ tsp coconut oil

To make the Chocolate Cream Cheese Frosting, place the chocolate in a microwave-safe bowl and melt in the microwave in 15-second increments, stirring in between, until completely melted. Set aside to cool.

In a large bowl, sift the powdered sugar with the cocoa powder and set aside. In a separate bowl, beat the cream cheese and butter with an electric mixer for 4 minutes, until creamy and fluffy. Add the melted and cooled chocolate and mix on low speed until combined, scraping the bowl as needed.

With the mixer off, add the sifted mixture. Mix on low speed until incorporated. Increase the speed to medium-high and beat the mixture for 1 minute. Add the vanilla and heavy cream and mix to combine. If you notice the frosting already has the perfect consistency, feel free to skip the addition of the cream. If the frosting still seems too thick, add another 1 or 2 teaspoons of cream, milk or water to thin it out. If the frosting is too runny, add some more sifted powdered sugar and mix until you achieve the desired consistency.

To make the Turtle Candy, line a baking sheet with parchment paper or a silicone mat. Create 18 to 20 clusters with 3 or 4 pecans each, depending on the size of the pecans. Place the unwrapped caramel candies in a microwave-safe bowl along with the heavy cream. Microwave the mixture in 15-second intervals, stirring in between, until the caramel is entirely melted and incorporated with the cream. Use a spoon to pour small amounts of caramel over the clusters of pecans, distributing it evenly among all the nuts. Let the caramel set for a few minutes.

In a microwave-safe bowl, melt the chocolate and coconut oil in the microwave in 15-second intervals, stirring in between, until completely melted and smooth. Pour the chocolate over the candies, distributing evenly among all the clusters. You can use a spoon to do this or you can place the chocolate in a piping bag and pipe it over the pecans. Let the candies sit until the chocolate and the caramel are set and dry. You can place them in the fridge to speed this up.

To assemble the cupcakes, remove the center of each cupcake with a spoon. Spoon the Pecan Caramel Filling into the middle of the cupcakes. Place the Chocolate Cream Cheese Frosting in a piping bag fitted with the tip of choice. Decorate the cupcakes with the frosting, and then place a Turtle Candy on top of each cupcake.

CASHEW TOFFEE CUPCAKES

There are not a lot of things in this world that I like more than toffee. The Vanilla Cupcakes are filled with Caramel Sauce and topped with Cashew Buttercream, in a creamy and rich combination that can only be improved by being topped with a piece of toffee candy. Using salted cashews to make the Cashew Toffee Candy will give a delicious touch of salty goodness to these indulgent treats.

Makes 14 cupcakes

VANILLA CUPCAKES

1½ cups (191 g) all-purpose flour

1 tsp baking powder

¼ tsp baking soda

¼ tsp fine sea salt

½ cup (113 g) unsalted butter, at room temperature

1 cup (200 g) granulated sugar

3 large eggs, at room temperature

1 tsp vanilla extract

½ cup (120 ml) milk, at room temperature

CASHEW TOFFEE CANDY

¾ cup (105 g) salted roasted cashews

½ cup (113 g) unsalted butter

½ cup (100 g) granulated sugar

⅛ tsp fine sea salt

¼ tsp vanilla extract

½ cup (85 g) finely chopped dark chocolate or chocolate chips

To make the Vanilla Cupcakes, preheat the oven to 350°F (177°C) and line 14 cupcake tins with cupcake liners.

In a large bowl, sift together the flour, baking powder, baking soda and salt. Set aside. In the bowl of an electric mixer, beat the butter on medium speed for about 1 minute. Add the granulated sugar and beat for 1 to 2 minutes, until creamy and fluffy. Scrape the sides of the bowl as necessary. Add the eggs, one at a time, mixing each egg until combined before adding the next. Add the vanilla, followed by the milk, and mix to combine. Lastly, add the dry ingredients and fold with a rubber spatula until incorporated.

Divide the batter evenly among the cupcake liners, filling them about two-thirds of the way. Bake for about 18 minutes. Start checking the cupcakes at the 15-minute mark, and keep baking and checking as necessary. To see if the cupcakes are ready, gently press with your finger on top of the cupcakes, and if they spring right back, that means they are done baking. Let the cupcakes cool completely before filling and frosting.

To make the Cashew Toffee Candy, line a 9 x 5–inch (23 x 13–cm) loaf pan with parchment paper. Spread the salted roasted cashews on the bottom of the pan. Set aside.

Place the butter, granulated sugar and salt in a small saucepan over medium heat and bring to a boil, stirring to help the sugar melt evenly. Once it comes to a boil, let the mixture simmer gently, and stir occasionally. Place a candy thermometer in the pan, and cook the caramel until it reaches 290°F (143°C). Remove it from the heat and stir the vanilla in carefully. Then, pour the caramel evenly over the cashews in the prepared pan. Let the toffee sit for 2 minutes.

Sprinkle the chopped chocolate on top of the toffee. Use a spatula to spread the chocolate as it melts, until it's completely smooth. Let the toffee set for 2 hours in the fridge. Slice it into small squares with a sharp knife.

(continued)

CARAMEL SAUCE

½ cup (100 g) granulated sugar

3 tbsp (42 g) unsalted butter

¼ cup (60 ml) heavy cream

CASHEW BUTTERCREAM

1 cup (226 g) unsalted butter, at room temperature

3 cups (375 g) powdered sugar, sifted

1 cup (150 g) ground cashews

1 tsp vanilla extract

1 tbsp (15 ml) heavy cream or milk, if needed

To make the Caramel Sauce, place the granulated sugar in a small saucepan over medium heat. Use a spatula to stir the sugar until it melts completely. Don't stop stirring; it's important to make sure the sugar is melting evenly. The melted sugar will start to have an amber color.

As soon as all the sugar melts and you see no more lumps of sugar, remove the pan from the heat and carefully add the butter. Stir until the butter melts. Then add the heavy cream. Be careful with this step, as the caramel will bubble up. Return the pan to the heat and cook the caramel for 1 minute over low heat. You are just looking to incorporate the sugar syrup with the butter and heavy cream. If you cook too long, the caramel will become hard as it cools.

Remove the caramel from the heat and pour it into a bowl. Let it come to room temperature before filling the cupcakes. If you make the caramel ahead, store it in the fridge and then reheat it gently for a few seconds in the microwave before filling the cupcakes.

To make the Cashew Buttercream, place the butter in the bowl of an electric mixer and cream it on medium-high speed for 4 minutes, until fluffy and creamy. Turn the mixer off and add the sifted powdered sugar and ground cashews. Mix on low speed to combine. Increase the speed to medium-high and beat for 1 minute, until smooth. Add the vanilla and mix to combine. If the buttercream is too stiff, add the heavy cream, 1 teaspoon at a time, to help smooth it out. If the buttercream is too runny, add more sifted powdered sugar, and mix until you obtain the desired consistency.

To assemble the cupcakes, remove the center of each cupcake with a spoon. Pour some Caramel Sauce into the middle of each cupcake. Place the Cashew Buttercream in a piping bag fitted with the tip of choice, and pipe it on top of the cupcakes. Finally, top each cupcake with a Cashew Toffee Candy.

The cupcakes can be stored in the refrigerator, covered, for up to 4 days.

CARAMEL CORN CUPCAKES

These treats will bring movie nights to a whole new level of deliciousness! Vanilla Cupcakes are filled with Salted Caramel Sauce, topped with Salted Caramel Buttercream and finished with Caramel Popcorn. They are buttery, sweet, fun and incomparable! Oh, and word of advice, you might want to make an extra batch of the Caramel Popcorn, just to be safe.

Makes 14 cupcakes

VANILLA CUPCAKES

1½ cups (191 g) all-purpose flour

1 tsp baking powder

¼ tsp baking soda

¼ tsp fine sea salt

½ cup (113 g) unsalted butter, at room temperature

1 cup (200 g) granulated sugar

3 large eggs, at room temperature

1 tsp vanilla extract

½ cup (120 ml) milk, at room temperature

SALTED CARAMEL SAUCE

½ cup (100 g) granulated sugar

3 tbsp (42 g) unsalted butter

¼ cup (60 ml) heavy cream

½ tsp kosher salt, or more to taste

To make the Vanilla Cupcakes, preheat the oven to 350°F (177°C) and line 14 cupcake tins with cupcake liners.

In a large bowl, sift together the flour, baking powder, baking soda and salt. Set aside.

In the bowl of an electric mixer, beat the butter on medium speed for about 1 minute. Add the granulated sugar and beat for 1 to 2 minutes, until creamy and fluffy. Scrape the sides of the bowl as necessary. Add the eggs, one at a time, mixing each egg until combined before adding the next. Add the vanilla, followed by the milk, and mix to combine. Lastly, add the dry ingredients and fold with a rubber spatula until incorporated.

Divide the batter evenly among the cupcake liners, filling them about two-thirds of the way. Bake for about 18 minutes. Start checking the cupcakes at the 15-minute mark, and keep baking and checking as necessary. To see if the cupcakes are ready, gently press with your finger on top of the cupcakes, and if they spring right back, that means they are done baking. Let the cupcakes cool completely before filling and frosting.

To make the Salted Caramel Sauce, place the granulated sugar in a small saucepan over medium heat. Use a spatula to stir the sugar until it melts completely. Don't stop stirring; it's important to make sure the sugar is melting evenly. The melted sugar will start to have an amber color. Remove the pan from the heat and carefully add the butter. Stir until the butter melts. Then add the heavy cream. Be careful with this step, as the caramel will bubble up. Return the pan to the heat, and cook the caramel for 1 minute over low heat. You are just looking to incorporate the sugar syrup with the butter and heavy cream. If you cook too long, the caramel will become hard as it cools.

Add the salt and stir to combine. Remove the caramel from the heat and pour it into a bowl. Let it come to room temperature before filling the cupcakes and making the buttercream. About ½ cup (130 g) of the sauce will be used to fill the cupcakes and the remaining ½ cup (130 g) will be used in the buttercream.

(continued)

SALTED CARAMEL BUTTERCREAM

1 cup (226 g) unsalted butter, at room temperature

½ cup (130 g) Salted Caramel Sauce

4 cups (500 g) powdered sugar, sifted

1 tsp vanilla extract

½ tsp kosher salt

CARAMEL POPCORN

2 tbsp (29 ml) neutral oil (if not using a popcorn popper)

⅓ cup (55 g) popcorn kernels

⅓ cup (75 g) unsalted butter

1 cup (200 g) light brown sugar

3 tbsp (45 ml) maple syrup, agave syrup or corn syrup

½ tsp fine sea salt

⅛ tsp cream of tartar

¼ tsp baking soda

To make the Salted Caramel Buttercream, place the butter in the bowl of an electric mixer. Beat the butter on medium-high speed for 5 minutes, until very creamy and fluffy, then add the Salted Caramel Sauce. Mix the caramel and butter on low speed for 30 seconds. Turn the mixer off and add the sifted powdered sugar. Mix on low speed until the sugar is completely incorporated. Increase the speed to medium-high and beat for 1 minute, until completely incorporated. Add the vanilla and salt and mix until combined and smooth. If the buttercream is too stiff, add 1 teaspoon of milk or water at a time and mix. If the buttercream is too soft, add some more sifted powdered sugar, mixing until you obtain the desired consistency.

To make the Caramel Popcorn, preheat the oven to 215°F (101°C). Line a baking sheet with parchment paper or a silicone mat.

Now, pop the popcorn. You will get about 8 cups (120 g) of popcorn from ⅓ cup (55 g) of kernels. You can use a popcorn popper, or you can easily make it on your stove. Simply add the oil to a large lidded pot with a heavy bottom. Place the pot over medium-high heat and throw two popcorn kernels in there. Close the lid. Wait a couple of minutes for the oil to heat. As soon as the two popcorn kernels pop, the oil is good to go. Pour all of the popcorn kernels in, pop the lid back on, and shake the pan slightly to distribute the kernels evenly on the bottom of the pan.

Let the kernels pop, occasionally shaking the pan to stir the kernels. After 30 seconds, open the lid of the pan slightly to allow some steam to escape. Place the lid back on and keep popping the corn until you only hear one pop every few seconds. When the popping slows down completely, the popcorn is done. Remove it from the heat and pour the popcorn onto the prepared baking sheet. Set aside.

Place the butter, brown sugar, maple syrup, salt and cream of tartar in a small saucepan. Bring the mixture to a boil over medium heat, stirring constantly. Let the mixture simmer for 2 minutes to thicken, stirring often. Remove it from the heat, add the baking soda and stir until combined. The caramel will get light in color and frothy.

Pour the sauce over the popcorn and stir with a spatula until completely combined. Transfer the popcorn to the oven and bake for a total of 60 minutes, stirring every 20 minutes. Remove from the oven and let it cool completely. Store in an airtight container at room temperature for up to 8 days.

To assemble the cupcakes, remove the center of each cupcake with a spoon. Pour some Salted Caramel Sauce into the middle of each cupcake. Place the Salted Caramel Buttercream in a piping bag fitted with the tip of choice, and pipe it on top of the cupcakes. Finally, top each cupcake with some Caramel Popcorn.

SALTED DULCE DE LECHE CUPCAKES

Dulce de leche is probably one of my favorite things in the whole world. I like eating it with a spoon right out of the jar, but I also enjoy baking with it. On my website, I have several dulce de leche recipes, so it's only fair I'd offer some here! These Chocolate Cupcakes feature Dulce de Leche Filling, because very few things in life go as well together as these two flavors. Topping the creation is a heavenly Salted Dulce de Leche Cream Cheese Frosting. The rich chocolate cake, the sweet and silky dulce de leche and the tangy cream cheese combo could only be improved by the addition of a touch of salt!

Makes 14 cupcakes

CHOCOLATE CUPCAKES

1½ cups (190 g) all-purpose flour

¼ cup (31 g) unsweetened cocoa powder

1 tsp espresso powder (optional)

1 tsp baking soda

¾ tsp baking powder

½ tsp fine sea salt

½ cup (120 ml) canola oil

1 cup (200 g) granulated sugar

1 cup (240 ml) brewed coffee or hot water

1 tbsp (15 ml) white vinegar

2 tsp (10 ml) vanilla extract

DULCE DE LECHE FILLING

1 (14-oz [397-g]) can condensed milk or 1 cup (300 g) store-bought dulce de leche, divided

To make the Chocolate Cupcakes preheat the oven to 350°F (177°C) and line 14 cupcake tins with cupcake liners.

In a large bowl, sift together the flour, cocoa powder, espresso powder (if using), baking soda, baking powder and salt; set aside.

In another bowl, mix together the oil, granulated sugar, coffee, vinegar and vanilla. Pour the dry mixture over the wet ingredients and whisk briefly, until incorporated. Be careful not to overmix. As soon as you see no more streaks of dry mixture, stop whisking.

Divide the batter evenly among the cupcake liners, filling them about two-thirds of the way. Bake the cupcakes for about 18 minutes. Start checking the cupcakes at the 15-minute mark, and keep baking and checking as necessary. To see if the cupcakes are ready, gently press with your finger on top of the cupcakes, and if they spring right back, that means they are done baking. Let the cupcakes cool completely before filling and frosting.

To make the Dulce de Leche Filling, preheat the oven to 350°F (177°C).

Pour the condensed milk into a small oven-proof bowl and cover it with foil. Place the bowl in a larger oven-proof pan, and fill the large pan with water to create a water bath. Bake the condensed milk in the oven for 2 to 3 hours, stirring every hour. Once the condensed milk has a deep caramel color and is thick, remove it from the oven. Let it cool completely, and preferably refrigerate it for a few hours before using it. Reserve ½ cup (150 g) of the dulce de leche to make the frosting.

(continued)

ESPRESSO WALNUT CREAM CUPCAKES

I want to put this Walnut Custard on absolutely everything! The custard is clearly the star of the recipe, absolutely scrumptious! Fluffy Espresso Cupcakes are filled with creamy Walnut Custard and topped with Espresso Walnut German Buttercream, then garnished with espresso beans. The combination of the rich custard and the espresso-flavored cupcakes makes this the perfect treat for tea time or afternoon coffee time.

Makes 14 cupcakes

ESPRESSO CUPCAKES

1½ cups (191 g) all-purpose flour

1 tsp espresso powder

1 tsp baking powder

¼ tsp baking soda

¼ tsp fine sea salt

½ cup (113 g) unsalted butter, at room temperature

1 cup (200 g) granulated sugar

3 large eggs, at room temperature

1 tsp vanilla extract

½ cup (120 ml) milk, at room temperature

WALNUT CUSTARD

¾ cup (180 ml) milk

½ cup (100 g) granulated sugar, divided

2 large egg yolks

2 tbsp (16 g) cornstarch

1 cup (125 g) ground walnuts

1 tsp vanilla extract

½ tbsp (7 g) unsalted butter

To make the Espresso Cupcakes, preheat the oven to 350°F (177°C) and line 14 cupcake tins with cupcake liners.

In a large bowl, sift together the flour, espresso powder, baking powder, baking soda and salt. Set aside.

In the bowl of an electric mixer, beat the butter on medium speed for about 1 minute. Add the granulated sugar and beat for another 1 to 2 minutes, until creamy and fluffy. Scrape the sides of the bowl as necessary. Add the eggs, one at a time, mixing each egg until combined before adding the next. Add the vanilla, followed by the milk, and mix to combine. Lastly, add the dry ingredients and fold with a rubber spatula until incorporated.

Divide the batter evenly among the cupcake liners, filling them about two-thirds of the way. Bake for about 18 minutes. Start checking the cupcakes at the 15-minute mark, and keep baking and checking as necessary. To see if the cupcakes are ready, gently press with your finger on top of the cupcakes, and if they spring right back, that means they are done baking. Let the cupcakes cool completely before filling and frosting.

To make the Walnut Custard, place the milk and ¼ cup (50 g) of the sugar in a small saucepan over medium heat and bring it to almost a boil, stirring so that the sugar melts. Turn off the heat before it actually comes to a boil.

Meanwhile, in a bowl, whisk the egg yolks with the remaining ¼ cup (50 g) of sugar and the cornstarch. Slowly pour about ¼ cup (60 ml) of the milk over the yolk mixture while whisking nonstop. Keep adding the remaining milk very slowly while whisking the custard. Once all the milk has been added to the yolks, return the whole mixture to the saucepan that you used to heat the milk, pouring it through a strainer to remove any bits of yolk that may have cooked. Add the ground walnuts to the custard.

(continued)

ESPRESSO WALNUT GERMAN BUTTERCREAM

½ cup (113 g) unsalted butter, at room temperature

1 cup (240 g) Walnut Custard

2½ to 3 cups (312 to 375 g) powdered sugar, sifted (see Note)

½ tsp espresso powder

Chocolate-covered espresso beans, for garnish (optional)

Place the pan over medium heat and cook, stirring nonstop with a wooden spoon or spatula, making sure to scrape the sides and bottom very well. The custard will start to get thick and it will look lumpy for a while, but just keep stirring over medium heat. After a couple of minutes, the mixture should be thick and smooth.

Remove the pan from the heat, add the vanilla and butter and stir to combine. Pour it into a small bowl and cover it with plastic wrap, placed right on the surface of the custard so it doesn't form a skin as it cools. Place it in the fridge to chill completely. Some of the Walnut Custard will be used to fill the cupcakes, and some will be used to make the buttercream.

To make the Espresso Walnut German Buttercream, place the butter in the bowl of an electric mixer and cream on medium-high speed for 4 minutes. Add 1 cup (240 g) of the chilled Walnut Custard and beat for 45 seconds. Turn off the mixer and add 2½ cups (312 g) of the sifted powdered sugar and the espresso powder. Mix on low speed until incorporated, then increase the speed to medium-high and beat for another minute, until creamy and thick. If the buttercream is too soft and runny, add more powdered sugar as necessary. If the buttercream is too stiff, add 1 to 2 teaspoons of milk or water to thin.

To assemble the cupcakes, use a spoon to remove the center of each cupcake. Fill the cupcakes with the Walnut Custard. Place the Espresso Walnut German Buttercream in a piping bag fitted with the tip of choice. Pipe the frosting on top of the cupcakes. Decorate with chocolate-covered espresso beans, if desired.

Note: The amount of powdered sugar used will depend on how thick you have cooked the custard. If your custard was on the runny side, you may need more powdered sugar.

ALMOND MATCHA CUPCAKES

Get a boost of energy with these Almond Matcha Cupcakes! Matcha is perfect for desserts, because it is slightly bitter yet smooth. The nutty and sweet almond flavor pairs so well with the matcha in this buttery and scrumptious fusion.

Makes 12 cupcakes

ALMOND CUPCAKES

1¼ cups (159 g) all-purpose flour

½ cup (48 g) almond flour

1¼ tsp (5 g) baking powder

½ tsp baking soda

½ tsp fine sea salt

½ cup (120 ml) vegetable oil

2 large eggs, at room temperature

¾ cup (150 g) granulated sugar

1 tsp vanilla extract

½ tsp almond extract

½ cup (120 ml) buttermilk, at room temperature

MATCHA CUSTARD

1 cup (240 ml) milk

⅓ cup (66 g) granulated sugar, divided

2 large egg yolks

2 tbsp (16 g) cornstarch

½ tsp matcha powder

1 tsp vanilla extract

2 tsp (10 g) unsalted butter

To make the Almond Cupcakes, preheat the oven to 350°F (177°C) and line 12 cupcake tins with cupcake liners.

In a large bowl, whisk together the all-purpose flour, almond flour, baking powder, baking soda and salt. Set aside.

In the bowl of an electric mixer, whisk the oil and eggs together until well combined. Add the granulated sugar and whisk for another minute, until smooth. Add the vanilla and almond extracts, followed by the buttermilk, and mix to combine. Lastly, add the dry ingredients and fold with a rubber spatula until incorporated.

Divide the batter evenly among the cupcake liners, filling them about two-thirds of the way. Bake for about 18 minutes. Start checking the cupcakes at the 15-minute mark, and keep baking and checking as necessary. To see if the cupcakes are ready, gently press with your finger on top of the cupcakes, and if they spring right back, that means they are done baking. Let the cupcakes cool completely before filling and frosting.

To make the Matcha Custard, place the milk and 3 tablespoons (36 g) of the sugar in a small saucepan. Bring it to almost a boil, turning the heat off right as you see the first bubbles emerging. Meanwhile, in a bowl, whisk the egg yolks with the remaining 2⅓ tablespoons (30 g) of sugar, the cornstarch and the matcha powder.

Add a couple of tablespoons (30 ml) of the hot milk to the yolk mixture while whisking. Once the first bit of milk has been whisked with the eggs, add a bit more, and do this until all the milk has been added to the yolks. Return the mixture to the saucepan, straining it through a fine-mesh sieve to remove any bits of cooked egg.

(continued)

MATCHA BUTTERCREAM

1½ cups (339 g) unsalted butter, at room temperature

3 cups (382 g) powdered sugar

2 tsp (4 g) matcha powder

1 tsp vanilla extract

⅛ tsp almond extract

2 tbsp (30 ml) milk

Whole or sliced toasted almonds, for garnish (optional)

Place the pan over medium heat and vigorously stir with a spatula or wooden spoon. Don't stop stirring at any point, or the eggs will cook on the bottom of the pan. Cook the custard for a few minutes. First it will start to look lumpy, and slowly, as you keep stirring, it will thicken and smooth out, becoming a rich and silky custard. When that happens, remove from the heat immediately, stir in the vanilla and butter and transfer the custard to a small bowl. Cover it with a piece of plastic wrap directly on top of the custard, so it doesn't form a skin as it cools. Place the custard in the fridge for a couple of hours until completely chilled.

To make the Matcha Buttercream, place the butter in the bowl of an electric mixer. Cream on medium-high speed for about 4 minutes, until very fluffy and lightened in color. Meanwhile, sift the powdered sugar and matcha powder together in a bowl.

With the mixer off, add the sifted mixture to the creamed butter. Mix on low speed until the sugar has incorporated with the butter. Increase the speed to medium-high and beat for about 1 minute. Add the vanilla and almond extracts and the milk and mix until combined. If the buttercream is too runny, add more sifted powdered sugar by the tablespoon (8 g), and mix to incorporate. If the buttercream is too stiff, add a bit more milk by the teaspoon, mixing in between, until you achieve a buttercream that is creamy, firm and smooth.

To assemble the cupcakes, use a spoon to remove the center of each cupcake. Spoon some of the Matcha Custard into the middle of the cupcakes. Place the Matcha Buttercream in a piping bag fitted with the piping tip of choice. Pipe the frosting over the cupcakes. Top with almonds, if desired.

The cupcakes can be stored in the refrigerator, covered, for up to 4 days.

ORANGE SEMOLINA CUPCAKES

Semolina flour provides a slightly grainy, yet chewy and soft texture to these super moist orange-flavored cupcakes. The filling is a sunny and bright Orange Marmalade, which is sweet, citrusy and somewhat tart. Everything is then brought together by the tangy and light Yogurt Frosting. To top these cupcakes, I made deliciously sticky Candied Oranges, which are so easy to make and such a huge hit.

Makes 14 cupcakes

SEMOLINA CUPCAKES

1¼ cups (200 g) fine semolina flour

½ cup (63 g) all-purpose flour

2 tsp (8 g) baking powder

¼ tsp baking soda

¼ tsp fine sea salt

½ cup (120 ml) olive oil

1 cup (200 g) granulated sugar

3 large eggs, at room temperature

1 tsp vanilla extract

⅔ cup (156 ml) milk, at room temperature

¼ cup (60 ml) orange juice

1 tbsp (5 g) orange zest

ORANGE MARMALADE

2 cups (280 g) peeled and chopped oranges

¼ cup (60 ml) water

½ cup (100 g) granulated sugar

2 tbsp (10 g) orange zest

To make the Semolina Cupcakes, preheat the oven to 350°F (177°C) and line 14 cupcake tins with cupcake liners.

In a large bowl, whisk together the semolina flour, all-purpose flour, baking powder, baking soda and salt. Set aside.

In a separate large bowl, whisk together the olive oil and granulated sugar for about 1 minute, until well incorporated. Add the eggs, one at a time, and whisk each egg until combined before adding the next. Add the vanilla, followed by the milk, orange juice and zest and whisk slowly. Add the dry ingredients to the bowl and stir with a spatula to combine.

Divide the batter evenly among the cupcake liners, filling them about two-thirds of the way. Bake for about 18 minutes. Start checking the cupcakes at the 15-minute mark, and keep baking and checking as necessary. To see if the cupcakes are ready, gently press with your finger on top of the cupcakes, and if they spring right back, that means they are done baking. Let the cupcakes cool completely before filling and frosting.

To make the Orange Marmalade, place the chopped oranges, water, granulated sugar and orange zest in a small saucepan over medium heat. Bring the mixture to a boil, and then lower the heat to medium-low. Stir the oranges regularly as you let them cook for about 40 minutes. If the marmalade begins to get dry, lower the heat and add a teaspoon of water or a splash of citrus juice (lemon or orange), and continue to cook until the mixture looks thick and glossy. Remove from the heat and let it cool. You may process it in a small blender to make it smooth, or use it with the chunks of oranges.

(continued)

YOGURT FROSTING

1 cup (226 g) unsalted butter,
at room temperature

½ cup (120 g) Greek yogurt

4¾ cups (593 g) powdered sugar,
sifted

1 tsp vanilla extract

CANDIED ORANGES

1 orange

½ cup (120 ml) water

½ cup (100 g) granulated sugar

To make the Yogurt Frosting, place the butter in the bowl of an electric mixer. Cream on medium-high speed for about 4 minutes, until very fluffy and lightened in color. Add the yogurt and mix until combined, scraping the bowl if necessary.

With the mixer on low, add the sifted powdered sugar to the creamed butter and yogurt. Mix on low speed until incorporated. Increase the speed to medium-high and beat for about 1 minute, until combined. Add the vanilla and mix until combined. If the buttercream is too runny, add more sifted powdered sugar by the tablespoon (8 g), and mix to incorporate. If the buttercream is too stiff, add a bit more yogurt, milk or water by the teaspoon, mixing in between, until you achieve a buttercream that is creamy, firm and smooth.

To make the Candied Oranges, line a baking sheet with a silicone mat or parchment paper. Slice the orange into ¼-inch (6-mm)-thick pieces, and then quarter each slice. Place the water and granulated sugar in a large pot. I like to use a large sauté pan to do this. Bring the water and sugar to a boil over high heat, and once the sugar has dissolved, lower the heat to medium and add the oranges to the pan. Try to keep them in an even layer, which is why it is helpful to use a large sauté pan.

Let the orange slices cook in the syrup for 20 minutes or so, until the syrup is very thick and the rind of the orange slices is almost translucent. Using a fork, remove one slice at a time, making sure to let each slice drip any excess syrup back into the pan. Place them on the prepared baking sheet and let them dry for a few hours, preferably overnight.

To assemble the cupcakes, use a spoon to remove the center of each cupcake. Spoon some Orange Marmalade into the middle of each cupcake. Place the Yogurt Frosting in a piping bag fitted with the tip of choice and pipe it on top of the cupcakes. Then decorate the cupcakes with the Candied Oranges.

The cupcakes can be stored in the refrigerator, covered, for up to 4 days.

TURMERIC LATTE CUPCAKES

Much like a golden ray of sunshine, these cupcakes are warm, feel-good treats that will brighten your day and boost your mood! Vanilla Cupcakes are infused with cozy spices, such as ginger, nutmeg and cinnamon, that complement the pungent and earthy turmeric flavor. Cupcakes with a side of bliss!

Makes 14 cupcakes

VANILLA CUPCAKES

1½ cups (191 g) all-purpose flour

1 tsp baking powder

¼ tsp baking soda

¼ tsp fine sea salt

¼ tsp ground cinnamon

¼ tsp ginger powder

⅛ tsp ground nutmeg

½ cup (113 g) unsalted butter, at room temperature

1 cup (200 g) granulated sugar

3 large eggs, at room temperature

1 tsp vanilla extract

½ cup (120 ml) milk, at room temperature

TURMERIC PASTRY CREAM

2 cups (480 ml) milk

¾ tsp ground turmeric

⅓ cup (66 g) granulated sugar, divided

2 egg yolks

3 tbsp (24 g) cornstarch

⅛ tsp ground ginger

1 tsp vanilla extract

1 tbsp (15 g) unsalted butter

To make the Vanilla Cupcakes, preheat the oven to 350°F (177°C) and line 14 cupcake tins with cupcake liners.

In a large bowl, sift together the flour, baking powder, baking soda, salt, cinnamon, ginger and nutmeg. Set aside.

In the bowl of an electric mixer, beat the butter on medium speed for about 1 minute. Add the granulated sugar and beat for another 1 to 2 minutes, until creamy and fluffy. Scrape the sides of the bowl as necessary. Add the eggs, one at a time, mixing each egg until combined before adding the next. Add the vanilla, followed by the milk, and mix to combine. Lastly, add the dry ingredients and fold with a rubber spatula until incorporated.

Divide the batter evenly among the cupcake liners, filling them about two-thirds of the way. Bake for about 18 minutes. Start checking the cupcakes at the 15-minute mark, and keep baking and checking as necessary. To see if the cupcakes are ready, gently press with your finger on top of the cupcakes, and if they spring right back, that means they are done baking. Let the cupcakes cool completely before filling and frosting.

To make the Turmeric Pastry Cream, combine the milk, turmeric and 3 tablespoons (36 g) of the granulated sugar in a small saucepan. Bring the mixture to almost a boil, stirring to help the sugar melt. As soon as you see the first bubbles emerging, remove from the heat. Meanwhile, add the yolks, remaining 2⅓ tablespoons (30 g) of the sugar, cornstarch and ginger to a bowl and whisk until combined.

Once you've removed the milk from the heat, slowly add a couple of tablespoons (30 ml) of the milk to the yolk mixture while whisking nonstop. Keep adding the remaining milk very slowly, whisking the custard. Once all the milk has been added to the yolks, return the whole mixture to the saucepan that you used to heat the milk, pouring it through a strainer to remove any bits of yolk that may have cooked.

(continued)

TURMERIC GERMAN BUTTERCREAM

½ cup (113 g) unsalted butter, at room temperature

¾ cup (186 g) Turmeric Pastry Cream

4 to 5 cups (500 g to 625 g) powdered sugar, sifted (see Note)

1 tsp vanilla extract

Place the pan over medium heat and cook, stirring nonstop with a wooden spoon or spatula, making sure to scrape the sides and bottom very well while you cook. The custard will start to get thick and it will look lumpy for a while, but just keep stirring over medium heat. After a couple of minutes, the mixture should be thick and smooth.

Remove the pan from the heat, add the vanilla and butter and stir to combine. Pour it into a small bowl and cover it with plastic wrap, placed right on the surface of the custard so it doesn't form a skin as it cools. Place it in the fridge to chill completely. Some of the pastry cream will be used to fill the cupcakes and some will be used to make the buttercream.

To make the Turmeric German Buttercream, beat the butter with an electric mixer on medium-high speed for 4 minutes, until fluffy and lightened in color. Add ¾ cup (186 g) of the chilled Turmeric Pastry Cream and cream it with the butter for 45 seconds. With the mixer off, add 4 cups (500 g) of the sifted powdered sugar to the bowl. Mix on low speed until incorporated, then increase the speed to medium-high and beat for another minute, until creamy and thick. Add the vanilla and mix to combine. If the buttercream is too soft and runny, add more powdered sugar as necessary. If the buttercream is too stiff, add 1 to 2 teaspoons of milk or water to thin.

To assemble the cupcakes, use a spoon to remove the center of each cupcake. Fill the cupcakes with the Turmeric Pastry Cream. Place the Turmeric German Buttercream in a piping bag fitted with the tip of choice. Pipe the frosting on top of the cupcakes.

The cupcakes can be stored in the refrigerator, covered, for up to 4 days.

Note: The amount of powdered sugar necessary will depend on how thick you have cooked the Turmeric Pastry Cream. If the pastry cream is on the runny side, you may have to add more powdered sugar as necessary.

ALMOND BUTTER GRANOLA CUPCAKES

Having cupcakes for breakfast just became totally acceptable with these Almond Butter Granola Cupcakes! They are topped with crunchy and nutty granola, to give some texture to the creamy and smooth cupcakes. The filling is simply almond butter, which goes so well with the tangy Almond Cream Cheese Frosting. For the nuts and seeds in the granola, I used a combination of chopped almonds, walnuts and pumpkin seeds. Feel free to use whatever nuts and seeds you have on hand.

Makes 12 cupcakes

ALMOND CUPCAKES

1¼ cups (159 g) all-purpose flour

½ cup (48 g) almond flour

1¼ tsp (5 g) baking powder

½ tsp baking soda

½ tsp fine sea salt

½ cup (120 ml) vegetable oil

2 large eggs, at room temperature

¾ cup (150 g) granulated sugar

1 tsp vanilla extract

½ tsp almond extract

½ cup (120 ml) buttermilk,
at room temperature

ALMOND CREAM CHEESE FROSTING

3 cups (375 g) powdered sugar

1 cup (96 g) almond flour

¾ cup (169 g) cream cheese,
at room temperature

¼ cup (56 g) unsalted butter

¼ cup (64 g) almond butter

1 tsp vanilla extract

¼ tsp almond extract

To make the Almond Cupcakes, preheat the oven to 350°F (177°C) and line 12 cupcake tins with cupcake liners.

In a large bowl, whisk together the all-purpose flour, almond flour, baking powder, baking soda and salt. Set aside.

In the bowl of an electric mixer, whisk the oil and eggs together until well combined. Add the granulated sugar and whisk for another minute, until smooth. Add the vanilla and almond extracts, followed by the buttermilk, and mix to combine. Lastly, add the dry ingredients and fold with a rubber spatula until incorporated.

Divide the batter evenly among the cupcake liners, filling them about two-thirds of the way. Bake for about 18 minutes. Start checking the cupcakes at the 15-minute mark, and keep baking and checking as necessary. To see if the cupcakes are ready, gently press with your finger on top of the cupcakes, and if they spring right back, that means they are done baking. Let the cupcakes cool completely before filling and frosting.

To make the Almond Cream Cheese Frosting, sift together the powdered sugar and almond flour into a bowl and set aside. In the bowl of an electric mixer, beat the cream cheese, butter and almond butter on medium-high speed for 4 minutes, until very fluffy and light in color, scraping the bowl once or twice during the process. Next, add the sifted mixture and mix on low speed until combined. Once incorporated, increase the speed to medium-high and beat for 1 more minute. Add the vanilla and almond extracts and mix to combine. If the frosting seems too thick, add 1 to 2 teaspoons of water or milk to thin it out, mixing as you go. If the frosting seems too thin, add some more sifted powdered sugar until you achieve the desired consistency.

(continued)

GRANOLA

½ cup (45 g) rolled oats

½ cup (60 g) chopped nuts and seeds of choice

¼ tsp fine sea salt

1 tbsp (15 ml) coconut oil

1½ tbsp (22 ml) maple syrup or honey

2 tbsp (12 g) dried fruit (such as cranberries, raisins or cherries) and/or semisweet chocolate chips

½ cup (128 g) almond butter, for filling

To make the Granola, preheat the oven to 350°F (177°C) and line a baking sheet with parchment paper or a silicone mat.

In a bowl, combine the oats, nuts and seeds, salt, coconut oil and maple syrup. Toss to coat well. Spread the mixture on the prepared baking sheet. Bake for 10 to 15 minutes, until lightly golden, stirring a couple of times in between. As soon as you remove the granola from the oven, add the dried fruit, stir and let cool.

To assemble the cupcakes, remove the center of each cupcake with a spoon. For the filling, spoon some almond butter into the middle of each cupcake. Place the Almond Cream Cheese Frosting in a large piping bag fitted with the tip of choice and pipe it over the cupcakes. Sprinkle some of the granola on top.

The cupcakes can be stored in the refrigerator, covered, for up to 4 days.

BROWN BUTTER EARL GREY CUPCAKES

In these exceptional cupcakes, you will find a noteworthy and surprising combo of brown butter and Earl Grey tea. The cupcakes are infused with brown butter and Earl Grey tea, which gives them a subtle yet remarkable aroma, enhanced by the fragrant Earl Grey Cream filling. For the frosting, we have a Brown Butter Buttercream, also lightly infused with Earl Grey, bringing together every single element of the cupcake in perfect harmony. The floral and citrusy Earl Grey notes pair nicely with the nutty brown butter, resulting in a decadent explosion of flavors that might just make these cupcakes one of your favorites from the chapter!

Makes 12 cupcakes

BROWN BUTTER

1 cup (226 g) unsalted butter

BROWN BUTTER EARL GREY CUPCAKES

⅓ cup (78 ml) milk

¾ tsp Earl Grey tea leaves or 1 Earl Grey tea bag

1⅓ cups (167 g) all-purpose flour

1 tsp baking powder

¼ tsp baking soda

¼ tsp fine sea salt

½ cup (113 g) Brown Butter, at room temperature

¾ cup (150 g) granulated sugar

3 large eggs, at room temperature

½ tsp vanilla extract

To make the Brown Butter, place the butter in a small saucepan over medium heat. Melt the butter and stir frequently as you bring it to a boil. Lower the heat and keep stirring the butter occasionally as you let it simmer gently for 5 to 7 minutes. The butter will be foaming up as the color deepens and starts to get golden. On the bottom of the pan, you will see the brown bits, which are milk solids from the butter caramelizing.

Remove the butter from the heat and pour it into a heatproof bowl. Let the butter come to room temperature completely before using it in the recipes. Half of the butter will be used for the cupcake batter, and the other half for the frosting. Make sure to stir the butter well before dividing it when it's time to make the cupcakes and the frosting, so you distribute the delicious bits of brown butter evenly.

To make the Brown Butter Earl Grey Cupcakes, preheat the oven to 350°F (177°C) and line 12 cupcake tins with cupcake liners.

Place the milk in a small saucepan and heat until it almost comes to a boil. Remove from the heat and add the tea leaves. Let it infuse for 10 minutes. Strain the milk, or remove the tea bag and discard. Let the milk come to room temperature before using.

In a large bowl, sift together the flour, baking powder, baking soda and salt; set aside. Place the Brown Butter in a bowl with the granulated sugar and cream with an electric mixer for 2 minutes, until well combined. Add the eggs, one at a time, mixing each egg until fully incorporated before adding the next. Add the vanilla and cooled infused milk and mix until incorporated. Lastly, add the sifted dry ingredients and fold with a rubber spatula until incorporated and smooth.

(continued)

EARL GREY CREAM

1 cup plus 3 tbsp (285 ml) milk

1 tsp Earl Grey tea leaves or 1 to 2 Earl Grey tea bags

⅓ cup (66 g) granulated sugar

2 large egg yolks

2 tbsp (16 g) cornstarch

2 tsp (10 g) unsalted butter

BROWN BUTTER BUTTERCREAM

½ cup (113 g) unsalted butter, at room temperature

½ cup (113 g) Brown Butter, at room temperature

4 cups (500 g) powdered sugar, sifted

3 tbsp (45 ml) Earl Grey–infused milk (from the Earl Grey Cream)

Sprinkles, for garnish (optional)

Divide the batter evenly among the cupcake liners, filling them about two-thirds of the way. Bake for about 18 minutes. Start checking the cupcakes at the 15-minute mark, and keep baking and checking as necessary. To see if the cupcakes are ready, gently press with your finger on top of the cupcakes, and if they spring right back, that means they are done baking. Let the cupcakes cool completely before filling and frosting.

To make the Earl Grey Cream, place the milk in a small saucepan and bring it almost to a boil over medium heat. Remove from the heat and add the tea leaves. Let it infuse for 10 minutes. Strain the milk, or remove the tea bag and discard. Let the milk come to room temperature before using.

Remove 3 tablespoons (45 ml) of the infused milk and set aside to use in the buttercream later. Reheat the remaining milk until hot. Meanwhile, in a bowl, whisk together the granulated sugar, egg yolks and cornstarch until the mixture is lightened in color. Slowly add just a couple of tablespoons (30 ml) of the hot milk to the mixture while whisking. Once the first bit of milk has been whisked with the eggs, add a bit more, and do this until all the milk has been added.

Return the mixture to the saucepan, straining it through a fine-mesh sieve to remove any bits of cooked egg. Place the pan over medium heat and stir vigorously with a spatula or wooden spoon. Don't stop stirring at any point, or the eggs will cook on the bottom of the pan. Cook the cream for a few minutes. First it will start to look lumpy, and slowly, as you keep stirring, it will thicken and smooth out, becoming a rich and silky custard. Remove from the heat immediately, stir in the butter and transfer the cream to a small bowl. Cover it with a piece of plastic wrap directly on top of the cream, so it doesn't form a skin as it cools. Place the cream in the fridge for a couple of hours until completely chilled.

To make the Brown Butter Buttercream, place the butter and Brown Butter in the bowl of an electric mixer. Cream on medium-high speed for 4 minutes, until creamy and fluffy. With the mixer off, add the sifted powdered sugar to the creamed butter. Mix on low speed until incorporated. Add the milk and keep mixing. Increase the speed to medium-high and beat for another minute, until creamy. If the buttercream seems too runny, add more powdered sugar. If the buttercream seems too stiff, add a teaspoon or so more milk, until you achieve the desired consistency.

To assemble the cupcakes, use a spoon to remove the center of each cupcake. Spoon some of the Earl Grey Cream into the middle of the cupcakes. Place the Brown Butter Buttercream in a piping bag fitted with the piping tip of choice. Pipe the frosting over the cupcakes and top with sprinkles, if using.

CHAI CLEMENTINE CUPCAKES

These Chai Cupcakes are filled with a delicious Clementine Compote and topped with a creamy Chai Spice Cream Cheese Frosting. The warming chai spices in the cupcake and the frosting form a delightful combination with the citrusy compote filling that will take you straight to tea time nirvana.

Makes 12 cupcakes

CHAI SPICE MIX

2 tsp (5 g) ground cinnamon

1¼ tsp (3 g) ground ginger

1¼ tsp (3 g) ground cardamom

½ tsp ground allspice

¼ tsp ground cloves

¼ tsp ground nutmeg

CHAI CUPCAKES

½ cup (120 ml) milk

1 chai tea bag

1½ cups (191 g) all-purpose flour

1 tsp baking powder

¼ tsp baking soda

¼ tsp fine sea salt

1 tbsp (8 g) Chai Spice Mix

¼ cup (56 g) unsalted butter, at room temperature

¼ cup (60 ml) vegetable oil

¾ cup (150 g) granulated sugar

2 large eggs, at room temperature

1 tsp vanilla extract

To make the Chai Spice Mix, in a bowl, combine the cinnamon, ginger, cardamom, allspice, cloves and nutmeg. If you don't care for a particular spice, feel free to replace it with another spice of your liking. For example, if you don't like cloves, add more allspice instead. The recipe makes 5½ teaspoons (13 g) of chai spice, which is how much we need for the whole recipe.

To make the Chai Cupcakes, preheat the oven to 350°F (177°C) and line 12 cupcake tins with cupcake liners.

In a saucepan over medium-high heat, bring the milk to almost a boil, turning the heat off as you see the first bubbles emerging. Place the tea bag in the milk and let it steep for 5 minutes. Remove the tea bag and let the milk cool to room temperature.

Meanwhile, in a large bowl, sift together the flour, baking powder, baking soda, salt and Chai Spice Mix. Set aside.

In the bowl of an electric mixer, beat the butter on medium speed for about 45 seconds. Add the oil and mix until incorporated. Add the granulated sugar and beat for another minute, until incorporated and creamy. Scrape the sides of the bowl as necessary. Add the eggs, one at a time, mixing each egg until combined before adding the next. Add the vanilla and mix. Make sure the milk is at room temperature, add it to the batter and mix until combined. Finally, add the sifted dry ingredients and fold with a rubber spatula until incorporated.

Divide the batter evenly among the cupcake liners, filling them about two-thirds of the way. Bake for about 18 minutes. Start checking the cupcakes at the 15-minute mark, and keep baking and checking as necessary. To see if the cupcakes are ready, gently press with your finger on top of the cupcakes, and if they spring right back, that means they are done baking. Let the cupcakes cool completely before filling and frosting.

(continued)

ESPRESSO MASCARPONE HONEY CUPCAKES

These cupcakes are like a triple shot of espresso! Mascarpone cheese is a buttery and rich fresh cream cheese, and it offers these cupcakes such a smooth quality to contrast with the bold flavors of the espresso and honey.

Makes 14 cupcakes

ESPRESSO HONEY CUPCAKES

1½ cups (191 g) all-purpose flour

1¼ tsp (5 g) baking powder

¼ tsp baking soda

¼ tsp fine sea salt

1 tsp espresso powder

½ cup (113 g) unsalted butter, at room temperature

¾ cup (180 ml) honey

2 large eggs, at room temperature

1 tsp vanilla extract

⅔ cup (156 g) Greek yogurt

HONEY ESPRESSO MASCARPONE FILLING

⅔ cup (150 g) mascarpone cheese

3 tbsp (45 ml) honey

½ tsp espresso powder

ESPRESSO MASCARPONE FROSTING

1 cup (240 ml) heavy cream, cold

¾ cup (93 g) powdered sugar, sifted

1 cup (226 g) mascarpone cheese, cold

1 tsp espresso powder

Bee pollen, for garnish (optional)

To make the Espresso Honey Cupcakes, preheat the oven to 350°F (177°C) and line 14 cupcake tins with cupcake liners.

In a large bowl, sift together the flour, baking powder, baking soda, salt and espresso powder. Set aside. In the bowl of an electric mixer, beat the butter on medium speed for about 1 minute. Add the honey and beat the mixture for another 1 to 2 minutes, until creamy and fluffy. Scrape the sides of the bowl as necessary. Add the eggs, one at a time, mixing each egg until combined before adding the next. Add the vanilla followed by the yogurt, and mix to combine. Add the dry ingredients to the bowl and fold with a rubber spatula until combined.

Divide the batter among the cupcake liners, filling them about two-thirds of the way. Bake the cupcakes for about 18 minutes. Start checking the cupcakes at the 15-minute mark, and keep baking and checking as necessary. To see if the cupcakes are ready, gently press with your finger on top of the cupcakes, and if they spring right back, that means they are done baking. Let the cupcakes cool completely before filling and frosting.

To make the Honey Espresso Mascarpone Filling, add the mascarpone cheese, honey and espresso powder to a small bowl and whisk until incorporated.

To make the Espresso Mascarpone Frosting, whip the heavy cream in a large bowl with an electric mixer on medium-high speed for 1 to 2 minutes, until soft peaks form. Add the sifted powdered sugar and mix briefly until combined. Add the mascarpone cheese and whip on medium-high speed for 2 minutes, or until you obtain stiff peaks. Add the espresso powder and mix briefly to combine, making sure not to overwhip the frosting. The frosting is best if piped immediately after it is made, but once it is piped it will hold its shape pretty well for a few days.

To assemble the cupcakes, use a spoon to remove the center of each cupcake. Spoon some of the Honey Espresso Mascarpone Filling into the middle of each cupcake. Place the Espresso Mascarpone Frosting in a piping bag fitted with the tip of choice. Pipe the frosting on top of the cupcakes. Sprinkle some bee pollen on top of the cupcakes to decorate, if desired.

Fall Vibes

On a crisp autumn afternoon, there's nothing more comforting than turning on the oven and filling your home with the scent of freshly baked cupcakes, brimming with warm spices and all the best fall flavors.

The cupcakes in this chapter will get you excited about the cooler weather with recipes featuring popular seasonal flavors such as maple, pumpkin and apple. Some of my favorites are the Walnut Streusel Pumpkin Cupcakes (page 155), Apple Bourbon Cupcakes (page 141) and Cranberry Gingerbread Cupcakes (page 147).

So grab your whisk, put on your fuzzy socks and get ready to bake some cupcakes. Then you will be ready to curl up under a blanket with a book and a treat. Isn't that what fall is all about?

MAPLE CINNAMON CUPCAKES

These Maple Cinnamon Cupcakes are for those who love fall days, cozy sweaters and eating cupcakes by the fireplace. And even if you don't have a fireplace, these cupcakes will warm you right up! The fluffy cupcakes are filled with Maple Cinnamon Custard and topped with sweet and rich Maple Buttercream.

Makes 16 cupcakes

MAPLE CINNAMON CUPCAKES

1¾ cups (223 g) all-purpose flour

1½ tsp (6 g) baking powder

½ tsp baking soda

¼ tsp fine sea salt

1 tsp ground cinnamon

½ cup (113 g) unsalted butter, at room temperature

1 cup (240 ml) maple syrup

2 large eggs, at room temperature

1 tsp vanilla extract

⅔ cup (156 g) sour cream

⅓ cup (78 ml) milk, at room temperature

MAPLE CINNAMON CUSTARD

1 cup (240 ml) milk

1 cinnamon stick (see Note on page 136)

2 large egg yolks

¼ cup (60 ml) maple syrup

2 tbsp (16 g) cornstarch

2 tsp (10 g) unsalted butter

To make the Maple Cinnamon Cupcakes, preheat the oven to 350°F (177°C) and line 16 cupcake tins with cupcake liners.

In a large bowl, sift together the flour, baking powder, baking soda, salt and cinnamon. Set aside.

In the bowl of an electric mixer, beat the butter on medium speed for about 1 minute. Add the maple syrup and beat for another 1 to 2 minutes, until creamy and fluffy. Scrape the sides of the bowl as necessary. Add the eggs, one at a time, mixing each egg until combined before adding the next. Add the vanilla, sour cream and milk and mix to combine. Lastly, add the dry ingredients and fold with a rubber spatula until incorporated.

Divide the batter evenly among the cupcake liners, filling them about two-thirds of the way. Bake for about 18 minutes. Start checking the cupcakes at the 15-minute mark, and keep baking and checking as necessary. To see if the cupcakes are ready, gently press with your finger on top of the cupcakes, and if they spring right back, that means they are done baking. Let the cupcakes cool completely before filling and frosting.

To make the Maple Cinnamon Custard, place the milk and cinnamon stick in a small saucepan. Bring the milk to almost a boil, turning the heat off right as you see the first bubbles emerging. Cover the pan and let the milk infuse for at least 30 minutes. Remove the cinnamon stick and heat the milk again over medium heat until hot.

Meanwhile, in a bowl, whisk together the egg yolks, maple syrup and cornstarch. Once the milk is hot, add a couple of tablespoons (30 ml) of the hot milk to the yolk mixture, whisking nonstop. Once the first bit of milk has been whisked with the eggs, add a bit more, and do this until all the milk has been added to the yolks. Return the mixture to the saucepan, straining it through a fine-mesh sieve to remove any bits of cooked egg.

(continued)

MAPLE BUTTERCREAM

1 cup (226 g) unsalted butter, at room temperature

⅓ cup (78 ml) maple syrup

4 cups (500 g) powdered sugar, sifted

Ground cinnamon, for garnish (optional)

Maple candies, for garnish (optional)

Place the pan over medium heat and vigorously stir with a rubber spatula or wooden spoon. Don't stop stirring at any point, or the eggs will cook on the bottom of the pan. Cook the custard for a few minutes. First it will start to look lumpy, and slowly, as you keep stirring, it will thicken and smooth out, becoming a rich and silky custard. When that happens, remove from the heat immediately, stir in the butter and transfer the custard to a small bowl. Cover it with a piece of plastic wrap directly on top of the custard, so it doesn't form a skin as it cools. Place the custard in the fridge for a couple of hours until completely chilled.

To make the Maple Buttercream, in a large bowl, beat the butter with an electric mixer on medium-high speed for 4 minutes. Add the maple syrup and mix to combine. Increase the speed and beat for another minute, until incorporated. Turn off the mixer, add the sifted powdered sugar and mix on low speed to combine. Increase the speed to medium and beat for 1 minute. If the buttercream is runny, add a bit more sifted powdered sugar. If the buttercream seems too stiff, add a teaspoon of water or milk at a time to adjust the consistency.

To assemble the cupcakes, remove the center of each cupcake with a spoon. Spoon some Maple Cinnamon Custard into the center of each cupcake. Place the Maple Buttercream in a piping bag fitted with the tip of choice, and pipe on top of the cupcakes. To decorate, sprinkle with cinnamon and top with maple candies, if desired.

The cupcakes can be stored in the refrigerator, covered, for up to 4 days. Let them come to room temperature slightly before serving.

Note: Feel free to skip the cinnamon stick and the infusing process and just add ½ teaspoon of ground cinnamon to the egg yolk mixture instead.

MAPLE GINGER CUPCAKES

These Maple Ginger Cupcakes are pretty much siblings to the Maple Cinnamon ones found on page 135. Both are perfect warming flavors for the colder seasons of the year. The Maple Ginger Cupcakes are a bit bolder, with a kick of spice provided by the ginger. You will find that the zesty ginger adds an exciting layer of flavor that just works so well with the sweet and decadent maple.

Makes 16 cupcakes

MAPLE GINGER CUPCAKES

1¾ cups (223 g) all-purpose flour

1½ tsp (6 g) baking powder

½ tsp baking soda

¼ tsp fine sea salt

½ cup (113 g) unsalted butter, at room temperature

1 cup (240 ml) maple syrup

2 large eggs, at room temperature

1 tsp vanilla extract

⅔ cup (156 g) sour cream

⅓ cup (78 ml) milk, at room temperature

1 tsp peeled and grated fresh ginger or ¼ tsp dry ground ginger

MAPLE GINGER CUSTARD

1 cup (240 ml) milk

¼ cup (28 g) chopped fresh ginger

2 large egg yolks

¼ cup (60 ml) maple syrup

2 tbsp (16 g) cornstarch

½ tsp dry ground ginger (optional)

2 tsp (10 g) unsalted butter

To make the Maple Ginger Cupcakes, preheat the oven to 350°F (177°C) and line 16 cupcake tins with cupcake liners.

In a large bowl, sift together the flour, baking powder, baking soda and salt. If using dry ground ginger, add it with the dry ingredients and sift it. Set aside.

In the bowl of an electric mixer, beat the butter on medium speed for about 1 minute. Add the maple syrup and beat for 1 to 2 minutes, until creamy and fluffy. Scrape the sides of the bowl as necessary. Add the eggs, one at a time, mixing each egg until combined before adding the next. Add the vanilla, sour cream and milk and mix to combine. Stir in the grated fresh ginger, if using. Lastly, add the dry ingredients and fold with a rubber spatula until incorporated.

Divide the batter evenly among the cupcake liners, filling them about two-thirds of the way. Bake for about 18 minutes. Start checking the cupcakes at the 15-minute mark, and keep baking and checking as necessary. To see if the cupcakes are ready, gently press with your finger on top of the cupcakes, and if they spring right back, that means they are done baking. Let the cupcakes cool completely before filling and frosting.

To make the Maple Ginger Custard, place the milk and ginger in a small saucepan. Bring the milk to almost a boil, turning the heat off right as you see the first bubbles emerging. Cover the pan and let the milk infuse with the ginger for at least 30 minutes. Strain it to remove the ginger and heat the milk again over medium heat until hot.

Meanwhile, in a bowl, whisk together the egg yolks, maple syrup and cornstarch. Once the milk is hot, add a couple of tablespoons (30 ml) of the hot milk to the yolk mixture, whisking nonstop. Once the first bit of milk has been whisked with the eggs, add a bit more, and do this until all the milk has been added to the yolks.

(continued)

BROWN SUGAR PUMPKIN CUPCAKES

These Brown Sugar Pumpkin Cupcakes are hearty and perfect for a cozy fall afternoon. Scrumptious Brown Sugar Cupcakes feature a creamy Pumpkin Filling and are topped with a Brown Sugar Italian Meringue Buttercream. Italian meringue buttercream tends to be on the light and less sweet side of the frosting spectrum, which is a quality that works perfectly well with the rich flavors present in these cupcakes, from the nutty and deep caramel notes provided by the brown sugar to the luscious pumpkin filling.

Makes 14 cupcakes

BROWN SUGAR CUPCAKES

1½ cups (191 g) all-purpose flour

1¼ tsp (5 g) baking powder

¼ tsp baking soda

¼ tsp fine sea salt

½ cup (113 g) unsalted butter, at room temperature

⅔ cup (133 g) packed brown sugar

2 tbsp (25 g) granulated sugar

3 large eggs, at room temperature

1 tsp vanilla extract

½ cup (120 ml) milk, at room temperature

PUMPKIN FILLING

¼ cup (60 ml) evaporated milk

1 cup (240 g) pumpkin puree

¼ cup (50 g) packed brown sugar

¼ tsp ground cinnamon

¼ tsp ground nutmeg

⅛ tsp fine sea salt

To make the Brown Sugar Cupcakes, preheat the oven to 350°F (177°C) and line 14 cupcake tins with cupcake liners.

In a large bowl, sift together the flour, baking powder, baking soda and salt. Set aside.

In the bowl of an electric mixer, beat the butter on medium speed for about 1 minute. Add the brown sugar and granulated sugar and beat for another 1 to 2 minutes, until creamy and fluffy. Scrape the sides of the bowl as necessary. Add the eggs, one at a time, mixing each egg until combined before adding the next. Add the vanilla, followed by the milk, and mix to combine. Add the dry ingredients and fold with a rubber spatula until combined.

Divide the batter among the cupcake liners, filling them about two-thirds of the way. Bake the cupcakes for about 18 minutes. Start checking the cupcakes at the 15-minute mark, and keep baking and checking as necessary. To see if the cupcakes are ready, gently press with your finger on top of the cupcakes, and if they spring right back, that means they are done baking. Let the cupcakes cool completely before filling and frosting.

To make the Pumpkin Filling, place the evaporated milk, pumpkin puree, brown sugar, cinnamon, nutmeg and salt in a small saucepan and bring to a boil over medium-high heat, stirring often. Let the mixture simmer for about 5 minutes, until thick. Remove to a small bowl and let it cool completely. Place in the fridge for at least 2 hours before using.

(continued)

BROWN SUGAR ITALIAN MERINGUE BUTTERCREAM

¾ cup (150 g) packed brown sugar

¼ cup (60 ml) water

4 large egg whites

1 cup (226 g) unsalted butter, cut into thin slices, at room temperature

1 tsp vanilla extract

Sprinkles, for garnish (optional)

To make the Brown Sugar Italian Meringue Buttercream, place the brown sugar and water in a small saucepan and attach a candy thermometer to the side of the pan. Bring to a boil over medium heat. Meanwhile, place the egg whites in the bowl of an electric mixer and whip them on low speed, gradually increasing the speed over the first minute, until you are whisking them on medium-high speed.

While the egg whites are beating and the syrup is cooking, keep your eye on both, as the syrup should achieve 240°F (115°C) and the eggs should form soft peaks at the same time. You might have to lower or raise the heat that's cooking the syrup to regulate it, or slow the speed at which you're beating the egg whites.

When the syrup achieves 240°F (115°C) on the thermometer, which is soft stage, pour it slowly over the soft peak meringue in the mixer. Decrease the speed of the mixer as you add the syrup, or the syrup will splatter everywhere, but keep it running, so the meringue doesn't immediately cook and curdle the egg whites. Once all the syrup has been added, increase the speed to medium-high and keep whipping until stiff peaks form and the bowl feels cool to the touch; this process can take up to 10 minutes.

When the meringue has achieved stiff peaks, start to slowly add the butter, one slice at a time, with the mixer on. Keep whipping until the buttercream looks creamy and fluffy and all the butter has been incorporated. This can take anywhere from 5 to 10 minutes, depending on the temperature of the butter and how well the meringue has been whipped. Finally, add the vanilla and mix until combined.

To assemble the cupcakes, remove the center of each cupcake with a spoon. Spoon some Pumpkin Filling into the center of each cupcake. Place the Brown Sugar Italian Meringue Buttercream in a piping bag fitted with the tip of choice and pipe over each cupcake. Top with some sprinkles, if using.

The cupcakes can be stored in the refrigerator, covered, for up to 4 days.

Troubleshooting Tips: If the buttercream is looking soupy, or doesn't seem to become fluffy and creamy, it might be for a couple of reasons. Number one: You didn't whip the meringue until stiff peaks were formed, and in this case, it will be very hard to get this buttercream to work and you mostly likely have to start over. Or it might be that your kitchen is too hot or the butter was too soft when you started to add it. In this case, place the bowl of the mixer in the freezer for about 5 minutes, then continue whipping, and your meringue will mostly likely start to get creamy and fluffy.

PEAR OLIVE OIL CUPCAKES

Olive oil cakes tend to be super moist and have an incredible crumb. Here, the olive oil provides an intense and rich flavor and pairs so well with the sweet Pear Butter filling. To frost the cupcakes, my choice is Stabilized Whipped Cream, which is light, fluffy and perfect to add some brightness while still letting the rich olive oil and pear combo shine!

Makes 12 cupcakes

OLIVE OIL CUPCAKES

1 cup (127 g) all-purpose flour

½ cup (48 g) almond flour

1 tsp baking powder

¼ tsp baking soda

¼ tsp fine sea salt

½ cup (120 ml) olive oil

¾ cup (150 g) granulated sugar

1 large egg, at room temperature

1 tsp vanilla extract

½ cup (120 ml) milk, at room temperature

PEAR BUTTER

2 cups (280 g) peeled and finely diced pears (about 3 pears)

2 tbsp (30 ml) honey

1 tbsp (15 ml) lemon juice

½ tsp peeled and grated ginger

½ tsp ground cardamom

To make the Olive Oil Cupcakes, preheat the oven to 350°F (177°C) and line 12 cupcake tins with cupcake liners.

In a large bowl, whisk together the all-purpose flour, almond flour, baking powder, baking soda and salt. Set aside.

In a separate large bowl, whisk together the olive oil and granulated sugar for about 1 minute, until well incorporated. Add the egg and whisk until combined, followed by the vanilla. Next, add the milk and whisk slowly. Add the dry ingredients to the bowl and fold with a rubber spatula to combine.

Divide the batter evenly among the cupcake liners, filling them about two-thirds of the way. Bake for about 18 minutes. Start checking the cupcakes at the 15-minute mark, and keep baking and checking as necessary. To see if the cupcakes are ready, gently press with your finger on top of the cupcakes, and if they spring right back, that means they are done baking. Let the cupcakes cool completely before filling and frosting.

To make the Pear Butter, add the pears, honey, lemon juice, ginger and cardamom to a small saucepan and bring to a boil over medium heat. Once the mixture reaches a boil, decrease the heat to medium-low and cover the pan. Continue to cook for 50 minutes, stirring occasionally and checking to make sure the mixture isn't getting too dry. If you notice the mixture is getting dry and sticking to the bottom of the pan, add a teaspoon of water and lower the heat. You should cook the Pear Butter until it looks thick, glossy and caramelized.

(continued)

STABILIZED WHIPPED CREAM

1 cup (226 g) cream cheese,
at room temperature

1 cup (125 g) powdered sugar, sifted

2¼ cups (540 ml) heavy cream, cold

1½ tsp (7 ml) vanilla extract

Green rock candy, for garnish
(optional)

To make the Stabilized Whipped Cream, in a bowl, beat the cream cheese with an electric mixer on medium-high speed for about 2 minutes, until smooth. Turn the mixer off and add the sifted powdered sugar to the cream cheese. Mix on low speed to combine, and then increase the speed to medium-high and beat for another minute.

With the mixer on low speed, pour in the heavy cream. Scrape the bowl, continue to mix on medium-low speed and slowly increase the speed to medium-high. Whip until the cream holds stiff peaks. Add the vanilla and mix briefly to combine. Remember, you don't want to keep beating the frosting after it reaches stiff peaks, because the whipped cream will curdle. Immediately pipe the frosting over the cupcakes. The frosting must be piped very soon after being made, or else it will begin to deflate. Once it is piped it will remain stable and firm.

To assemble the cupcakes, remove the center of each cupcake with a spoon. Spoon some Pear Butter into the center of each cupcake. Place the Stabilized Whipped Cream in a piping bag fitted with the tip of choice and pipe over each cupcake. Decorate the cupcakes with some green rock candy, if desired.

The cupcakes can be stored in the refrigerator, covered, for up to 4 days.

ROASTED RHUBARB CUPCAKES

These Roasted Rhubarb Cupcakes are the perfect late spring, early summer treat, when you start to see rhubarb at the stores and farmers' markets! The tangy and sour Roasted Rhubarb Filling cuts right through the rich and sweet Vanilla Bean Cream Cheese Frosting, making this an ethereal combination!

Makes 14 cupcakes

VANILLA CUPCAKES

1½ cups (191 g) all-purpose flour

1 tsp baking powder

¼ tsp baking soda

¼ tsp fine sea salt

½ cup (113 g) unsalted butter, at room temperature

1 cup (200 g) granulated sugar

3 large eggs, at room temperature

1 tsp vanilla extract

½ cup (120 ml) milk, at room temperature

ROASTED RHUBARB FILLING

3 cups (300 g) sliced rhubarb, cut into 1-inch (2.5-cm) pieces, plus more for garnish

¼ cup (50 g) granulated sugar

1 tbsp (15 ml) lemon juice

3 mint leaves

To make the Vanilla Cupcakes, preheat the oven to 350°F (177°C) and line 14 cupcake tins with cupcake liners.

In a large bowl, sift together the flour, baking powder, baking soda and salt. Set aside.

In the bowl of an electric mixer, beat the butter on medium speed for about 1 minute. Add the granulated sugar and beat for another 1 to 2 minutes, until creamy and fluffy. Scrape the sides of the bowl as necessary. Add the eggs, one at a time, mixing each egg until combined before adding the next. Add the vanilla, followed by the milk, and stir to combine. Lastly, add the dry ingredients and fold with a rubber spatula until incorporated.

Divide the batter evenly among the cupcake liners, filling them about two-thirds of the way. Bake for about 18 minutes. Start checking the cupcakes at the 15-minute mark, and keep baking and checking as necessary. To see if the cupcakes are ready, gently press with your finger on top of the cupcakes, and if they spring right back, that means they are done baking. Let the cupcakes cool completely before filling and frosting.

To make the Roasted Rhubarb Filling, preheat the oven to 300°F (148°C). Line a baking sheet with parchment paper or a silicone mat.

Put the rhubarb, granulated sugar, lemon juice and mint leaves in a bowl and gently stir to combine. Spread the rhubarb on the prepared baking sheet in an even layer. Roast for about 20 minutes, stirring occasionally, until the rhubarb has softened and the syrup is caramelized. Remove from the oven and transfer to a glass bowl. Discard the mint leaves, as they are just used to infuse the rhubarb with the mint flavor. Let the mixture chill in the fridge for at least 2 hours.

(continued)

VANILLA BEAN CREAM CHEESE FROSTING

1 cup (226 g) cream cheese, at room temperature

½ cup (113 g) unsalted butter, at room temperature

1 vanilla bean (see Note)

4 cups (500 g) powdered sugar, sifted

To make the Vanilla Bean Cream Cheese Frosting, place the cream cheese and butter in the bowl of an electric mixer. Cream on medium-high speed for 4 minutes, until very fluffy and light in color, scraping the bowl once or twice during the process.

Slice the vanilla bean lengthwise and use the back of a paring knife to scrape the seeds into the bowl. Mix on medium-high speed for a few seconds to incorporate the vanilla bean. Next, add the sifted powdered sugar to the cream cheese mixture. Mix on low speed until combined. Once incorporated, increase the speed to medium-high and beat for 1 more minute.

To assemble the cupcakes, remove the center of each cupcake with a spoon. Next, spoon some Roasted Rhubarb Filling into the middle of each cupcake. Place the Vanilla Bean Cream Cheese Frosting in a piping bag fitted with the piping tip of choice. Pipe on top of the cupcakes. Decorate the cupcakes with a piece of rhubarb, if desired.

The cupcakes can be stored in the refrigerator, covered, for up to 4 days.

Note: If you don't want to use a vanilla bean, feel free to use 1 teaspoon of vanilla extract instead, and add it to the frosting after adding the powdered sugar.

KEY LIME PIE CUPCAKES

These Key Lime Pie Cupcakes are inspired by my favorite childhood pie! They are filled with a Key Lime Pie Filling that tastes exactly like the pie you'd get at a bakery, and then topped with Marshmallow Frosting that is toasted with a kitchen torch. You will wonder where these cupcakes have been your whole life!

Key limes are usually the small limes and have a stronger, more pronounced acidic flavor. If you can't find Key limes, regular limes will work just fine.

Makes 14 cupcakes

KEY LIME CUPCAKES

1½ cups (191 g) all-purpose flour

1 tsp baking powder

¼ tsp baking soda

¼ tsp fine sea salt

½ cup (120 ml) vegetable oil

2 eggs, at room temperature

¾ cup (150 g) granulated sugar

1 tsp vanilla extract

½ cup (120 ml) milk, at room temperature

⅓ cup (78 ml) Key lime juice

2 tbsp (10 g) Key lime zest

KEY LIME PIE FILLING

½ cup (113 g) cream cheese, at room temperature

¼ cup (60 ml) condensed milk

1½ tbsp (22 ml) Key lime juice

1 tbsp (5 g) Key lime zest

To make the Key Lime Cupcakes, preheat the oven to 350°F (177°C) and line 14 cupcake tins with cupcake liners.

In a large bowl, sift together the flour, baking powder, baking soda and salt; set aside.

In a separate large bowl, whisk together the oil and eggs. Add the granulated sugar and whisk until combined. Add the vanilla, milk, lime juice and zest and whisk. Lastly, add the sifted dry ingredients and fold with a rubber spatula until incorporated and smooth.

Divide the batter evenly among the cupcake liners, filling them about two-thirds of the way. Bake for about 18 minutes. Start checking the cupcakes at the 15-minute mark, and keep baking and checking as necessary. To see if the cupcakes are ready, gently press with your finger on top of the cupcakes, and if they spring right back, that means they are done baking. Let the cupcakes completely cool before filling and frosting.

To make the Key Lime Pie Filling, beat the cream cheese with an electric mixer on medium-high speed for 3 minutes, until creamy and fluffy. Add the condensed milk and continue to beat for another minute. Lastly, add the lime juice and zest and cream until well combined and smooth.

(continued)

MARSHMALLOW FROSTING

4 large egg whites

1 cup (200 g) granulated sugar

¼ tsp cream of tartar

¼ tsp fine sea salt

1 tsp vanilla extract

1 oz (28 g) graham cracker crumbs, for garnish (optional)

To make the Marshmallow Frosting, combine the egg whites, granulated sugar, cream of tartar and salt in a heatproof bowl. Set the bowl over a pot of barely simmering water to form a double boiler. Make sure the water isn't boiling, and make sure the bottom of the bowl isn't touching the water surface, because we don't want the egg whites to cook.

Whisk the mixture for a few minutes until it reaches 140°F (60°C) on a candy thermometer. Once the syrup achieves this temperature and the sugar is completely melted, remove the bowl from the double boiler. Whip the syrup with an electric mixer fitted with the whisk attachment for about 5 minutes on high speed. Add the vanilla and mix to combine. The frosting should have stiff peaks and be fluffy, glossy and white.

To assemble the cupcakes, use a spoon to remove the center of each cupcake. Spoon or pipe the Key Lime Pie Filling into the middle of each cupcake. Place the Marshmallow Frosting in a piping bag fitted with the tip of choice. Pipe the frosting on top of each cupcake. You can use a kitchen torch to toast the frosting for a finishing touch. Sprinkle the cupcakes with graham cracker crumbs to decorate, if desired.

The cupcakes can be stored in the refrigerator, covered, for up to 4 days.

BLOOD ORANGE THYME CUPCAKES

This combo has a delicate, earthy layer of flavor, lent by the Thyme Cupcakes and complemented by the sweet and citrusy Blood Orange Curd filling. To top the cupcakes, I chose Cream Cheese Frosting for its tangy and creamy qualities. You may not want to even share these with anybody, but if you do, know that they will be the star of any dessert table.

Makes 14 cupcakes

THYME CUPCAKES

1½ cups (191 g) all-purpose flour

1 tsp baking powder

¼ tsp baking soda

¼ tsp fine sea salt

½ cup (120 ml) milk, at room temperature

1 tbsp (15 ml) blood orange juice

½ cup (113 g) unsalted butter, at room temperature

1 cup (200 g) granulated sugar

3 large eggs, at room temperature

1 tsp vanilla extract

2 tsp (2 g) fresh thyme leaves

1 tbsp (5 g) blood orange zest

BLOOD ORANGE CURD

¼ cup (56 g) unsalted butter, at room temperature

⅓ cup plus 1 tbsp (79 g) granulated sugar

2 large eggs

⅓ cup (78 ml) blood orange juice

3 tbsp (15 g) blood orange zest

¼ tsp salt

To make the Thyme Cupcakes, preheat the oven to 350°F (177°C) and line 14 cupcake tins with cupcake liners.

In a large bowl, sift together the flour, baking powder, baking soda and salt; set aside. In a small bowl, combine the milk and blood orange juice and set aside.

Meanwhile, in the bowl of an electric mixer, beat the butter on medium speed for about 1 minute. Add the granulated sugar and beat for another 1 to 2 minutes, until creamy and fluffy. Scrape the sides of the bowl as necessary. Add the eggs, one at a time, mixing each egg until combined before adding the next. Add the vanilla, followed by the milk mixture, and stir to combine. Lastly, add the thyme leaves, blood orange zest and the dry ingredients and fold with a rubber spatula until incorporated.

Divide the batter evenly among the cupcake liners, filling them about two-thirds of the way. Bake for about 18 minutes. Start checking the cupcakes at the 15-minute mark, and keep baking and checking as necessary. To see if the cupcakes are ready, gently press with your finger on top of the cupcakes, and if they spring right back, they are done baking. Let the cupcakes cool completely before filling and frosting.

To make the Blood Orange Curd, in a bowl, beat the butter with an electric mixer for 1 minute. Add the granulated sugar and beat for another minute. Next, add the eggs, one at a time, mixing each egg until combined before adding the next. Add the blood orange juice, zest and salt and mix on low speed until combined. The mixture might look separated and that's okay. Pour it into a small saucepan and place over medium-low heat. Don't let the curd come to a boil, and don't stop stirring at any point either, because that will lead to the eggs curdling.

Heat the curd slowly until a candy thermometer reads 170°F (76°C). The curd should be thick and coat the back of a spoon. Once you achieve a nice thick curd, remove it to a bowl and place it in the fridge for at least 2 hours; the curd will set and get very thick as it cools.

(continued)

CREAM CHEESE FROSTING

1 cup (226 g) cream cheese,
at room temperature

½ cup (113 g) unsalted butter,
at room temperature

4 cups (500 g) powdered sugar,
sifted

1½ tsp (7 ml) vanilla extract

To make the Cream Cheese Frosting, place cream cheese and butter in the bowl of an electric mixer. Cream on medium-high speed for 4 minutes, until very fluffy and light in color, scraping the bowl once or twice during the process. Next, add the sifted powdered sugar to the cream cheese and butter. Mix on low speed until combined. Once incorporated, increase the speed to medium-high and beat for 1 more minute. Add the vanilla and mix to combine.

To assemble the cupcakes, remove the center of each cupcake with a spoon. Next, spoon some Blood Orange Curd into the middle of each cupcake. Alternatively, you can place the curd in a piping bag, snip the end with scissors and pipe the curd into the center of the cupcakes. Place the Cream Cheese Frosting in a piping bag fitted with the piping tip of choice. Pipe a tall ring around the edge of the cupcakes, leaving a hole in the middle. Spoon or pipe some more curd into the middle of the frosting ring.

The cupcakes can be stored in the refrigerator, covered, for up to 4 days.

BLUEBERRY RICOTTA CUPCAKES

These Blueberry Ricotta Cupcakes are one of the easiest to make in the book. The soft Ricotta Cupcakes have a hint of almond flavor and are filled with a delicious Blueberry Jam. The Ricotta Frosting draws all the elements together, making these cupcakes sophisticated and enjoyable.

Makes 14 cupcakes

RICOTTA CUPCAKES

1½ cups (191 g) all-purpose flour

1 tsp baking powder

¼ tsp baking soda

¼ tsp fine sea salt

½ cup (113 g) unsalted butter, at room temperature

1 cup (200 g) granulated sugar

3 large eggs, at room temperature

1 tsp vanilla extract

⅛ tsp almond extract

½ cup (123 g) whole milk ricotta, at room temperature

BLUEBERRY JAM

2 cups (280 g) blueberries, plus more for garnish (optional)

2 tbsp (25 g) granulated sugar

2 tbsp (30 ml) lemon juice

1 tsp cornstarch

2 tsp (10 ml) water

To make the Ricotta Cupcakes, preheat the oven to 350°F (177°C) and line 14 cupcake tins with cupcake liners.

In a large bowl, sift together the flour, baking powder, baking soda and salt. Set aside.

In the bowl of an electric mixer, beat the butter on medium speed for about 1 minute. Add the granulated sugar and beat for another 1 to 2 minutes, until creamy and fluffy. Scrape the sides of the bowl as necessary. Add the eggs, one at a time, mixing each egg until combined before adding the next. Add the vanilla and almond extracts, followed by the ricotta, and mix to combine. Lastly, add the sifted dry ingredients and fold with a rubber spatula until incorporated.

Divide the batter evenly among the cupcake liners, filling them about two-thirds of the way. Bake for about 18 minutes. Start checking the cupcakes at the 15-minute mark, and keep baking and checking as necessary. To see if the cupcakes are ready, gently press with your finger on top of the cupcakes, and if they spring right back, that means they are done baking. Let the cupcakes cool completely before filling and frosting.

To make the Blueberry Jam, place the blueberries, granulated sugar and lemon juice in a small saucepan. Cook the blueberries over medium heat for about 15 minutes, until they become softened and are falling apart. Make sure to stir the mixture every so often, and if it gets too dry as it cooks, add 1 teaspoon of water and lower the heat. In a small bowl, mix the cornstarch with the water until dissolved, then add it to the pan. Keep stirring and cooking the jam until it thickens, about 2 minutes. Transfer the jam to a bowl, cover and refrigerate until thoroughly chilled.

(continued)

RICOTTA FROSTING

½ cup (113 g) unsalted butter,
at room temperature

⅔ cup (162 g) whole milk ricotta

3 cups (375 g) powdered sugar,
sifted

½ tsp vanilla extract

To make the Ricotta Frosting, beat the butter with an electric mixer for 3 minutes on medium-high speed, until creamy and fluffy. Add the ricotta and cream on medium speed for another minute, until incorporated. With the mixer off, add the sifted powdered sugar to the bowl with the butter and ricotta. Mix on low speed until the mixture is incorporated. Increase the speed to medium-high and beat for another minute. Add the vanilla and mix to combine.

To assemble the cupcakes, use a spoon to remove the center of each cupcake. Spoon some of the Blueberry Jam into the middle of the cupcakes. Place the Ricotta Frosting in a piping bag fitted with the piping tip of choice. Pipe the frosting over the cupcakes. Top with some blueberries, if desired.

The cupcakes can be stored in the refrigerator, covered, for up to 4 days.

Note: You can also use store-bought jam for this recipe. You will need about 1 cup (240 g).

BALSAMIC ROASTED STRAWBERRY CUPCAKES

Looking for a lavish cupcake option to serve to your fanciest guests? Go with these Balsamic Roasted Strawberry Cupcakes! Vanilla Cupcakes are filled with sweet and tangy Balsamic Roasted Strawberries, and then topped with an airy Balsamic Caramel Swiss Meringue Buttercream. These cupcakes are truly suitable for elevated palates!

Makes 14 cupcakes

VANILLA CUPCAKES

1½ cups (191 g) all-purpose flour

1 tsp baking powder

¼ tsp baking soda

¼ tsp fine sea salt

½ cup (113 g) unsalted butter, at room temperature

1 cup (200 g) granulated sugar

3 large eggs, at room temperature

1 tsp vanilla extract

½ cup (120 ml) milk, at room temperature

BALSAMIC ROASTED STRAWBERRIES

3⅓ cups (500 g) quartered strawberries

3 tbsp (37 g) granulated sugar

3 tbsp (45 ml) balsamic vinegar

BALSAMIC CARAMEL SAUCE

¼ cup (50 g) packed light brown sugar

2 tbsp (30 ml) balsamic vinegar

⅛ tsp salt

½ tbsp (7 g) unsalted butter

¼ cup (60 ml) heavy cream

To make the Vanilla Cupcakes, preheat the oven to 350°F (177°C) and line 14 cupcake tins with cupcake liners.

In a large bowl, sift together the flour, baking powder, baking soda and salt. Set aside.

In the bowl of an electric mixer, beat the butter on medium speed for about 1 minute. Add the granulated sugar and beat for another 1 to 2 minutes, until creamy and fluffy. Scrape the sides of the bowl as necessary. Add the eggs, one at a time, mixing each egg until combined before adding the next. Add the vanilla, followed by the milk, and mix to combine. Lastly, add the dry ingredients and fold with a rubber spatula until incorporated.

Divide the batter evenly among the cupcake liners, filling them about two-thirds of the way. Bake for about 18 minutes. Start checking the cupcakes at the 15-minute mark, and keep baking and checking as necessary. To see if the cupcakes are ready, gently press with your finger on top of the cupcakes, and if they spring right back, they are done baking. Let the cupcakes cool completely before filling and frosting.

To make the Balsamic Roasted Strawberries, preheat the oven to 300°F (148°C). Line a baking sheet with parchment paper or a silicone mat.

Put the strawberries, granulated sugar and vinegar in a bowl and gently stir to combine. Spread the strawberries on the prepared baking sheet in an even layer. Roast for about 20 minutes, stirring occasionally, until the strawberries have softened and the syrup coating them is caramelized. Remove from the oven, transfer to a glass bowl and chill in the fridge for at least 2 hours.

To make the Balsamic Caramel Sauce, place the brown sugar and balsamic vinegar in a small saucepan over medium heat. Use a spatula to stir the sugar until it melts completely. Don't stop stirring; it's important to make sure the sugar is melting evenly. The melted sugar will start to have an amber color.

(continued)

MARSHMALLOW FROSTING

4 large egg whites

1 cup (200 g) granulated sugar

¼ tsp cream of tartar

¼ tsp fine sea salt

1 tsp vanilla extract

Fresh passion fruit seeds, for garnish (optional)

To make the Marshmallow Frosting, beat the egg whites, granulated sugar, cream of tartar and salt in a heat proof bowl. Set the bowl over a pot of barely simmering water to form a double boiler. Make sure the water isn't boiling, and make sure the bottom of the bowl isn't touching the water surface. Whisk the mixture for a few minutes over the barely simmering water until it reaches 140°F (60°C) on a candy thermometer.

Once the syrup achieves this temperature and the sugar is completely melted, remove the bowl from the double boiler. Whip the syrup with an electric mixer fitted with the whisk attachment on high speed for about 5 minutes. Add the vanilla and mix to combine. The meringue should have stiff peaks and be fluffy, glossy and white.

To assemble the cupcakes, use a spoon to remove the center of each cupcake. Spoon some of the Passion Fruit Curd into the middle of each cupcake. Place the Marshmallow Frosting in a piping bag fitted with the tip of choice. Pipe a ring around each cupcake, leaving space in the center so you can fill it up to the top with some more curd. Pipe (or spoon) more curd into the center of the piped frosting.

You can use a blowtorch to toast the Marshmallow Frosting; this is optional, but I think it's a nice touch to finish off these cupcakes. If you are able to find some fresh passion fruit, spoon some seeds on top of the curd.

The cupcakes can be stored in the refrigerator, covered, for up to 3 days.

Note: Make sure the passion fruit pulp you are using is unsweetened. If you use sweetened passion fruit pulp for this recipe, omit the sugar so the curd is not overly sweet. If you can't find fresh passion fruit at your grocery store, you can easily find the pulp in the frozen aisle of most stores or online.

ACKNOWLEDGMENTS

Thank you! I have to first and foremost acknowledge my husband, who has supported me since before I even started my career as a recipe developer and food photographer. Brian, thank you for motivating me to follow my passion. Thank you for washing countless dishes, for saying encouraging words, for cheering me on along the way, for celebrating with excitement every time I accomplish a goal or tackle a task, and for always saying, "Just tell me what I can do to help." Those words alone are such a huge help already!

My favorite boy in the whole world, my son Luke, thank you for being patient, for being my buddy in the kitchen, my little baker in the making. Your presence, lightness and smile are always what I turn to when I need a sparkle to keep going!

Mom and Dad, Mãe e Pai, thank you for trusting me and my dreams and for being there for me unconditionally. Even though you are thousands of miles away, it feels like you are so close. Thank you for giving me everything I needed to be who I am today.

My sisters, Aline and Marina, my stars, thank you for being my best friends, for being my cheerleaders and my support system. You are the reason why I do this!

To my grandparents on my mom's side, for teaching me diligence and a love for baking. And my grandma on my dad's side, for cultivating in me the joy behind cooking and sharing with loved ones!

Thank you also to my Tía Rosy, for being such a rock and such an inspiration.

The team at Page Street Publishing, thank you for this opportunity to work on an amazing project and for allowing me to share my passion in this beautiful book!

Thank you to Emily Taylor, my editor, for being so sweet, helpful and understanding and for believing in me!

And a huge and special thanks to my readers and followers, who show me unequivocal support and love every day! Thanks to the amazing online baking community for inspiring me, and holding a safe and beautiful space where I could create a sense of belonging that feels as warm and comforting as my kitchen while my oven is on baking cupcakes.

ABOUT THE AUTHOR

Camila Hurst is a self-taught baker, born and raised in Brazil. She moved to the United States in 2011 and turned her baking hobby into a successful and thriving career as a recipe developer and food photographer. Her blog Pies and Tacos focuses on fabulous desserts baked from scratch. Camila is also a children's book author. She lives in beautiful upstate New York with her husband and son.

INDEX